WABI
SABI
HOME

WABI
SABI
HOME

FINDING BEAUTY
IN IMPERFECTION

MARK & SALLY BAILEY
PHOTOGRAPHY BY DEBI TRELOAR

RYLAND PETERS & SMALL
LONDON • NEW YORK

SENIOR DESIGNER Megan Smith
SENIOR COMMISSIONING EDITOR
Annabel Morgan
LOCATION MANAGER Jess Walton
PRODUCTION MANAGER
Gordana Simakovic
ART DIRECTOR Leslie Harrington
EDITORIAL DIRECTOR Julia Charles
PUBLISHER Cindy Richards

STYLING Mark Bailey
INDEXER Diana LeCore

First published in 2014 as
Imperfect Home.
This edition published by
Ryland Peters & Small
20–21 Jockey's Fields,
London WC1R 4BW
and
341 E 116th Street
New York, NY 10029

www.rylandpeters.com

10 9 8 7 6 5 4 3 2 1

Text © Mark and Sally Bailey 2014, 2019
Design and photographs
© Ryland Peters & Small 2014, 2019

ISBN: 978-1-78879-091-8

Printed and bound in China

CONTENTS

This book was inspired by a hand-beaten brass spoon, bought from Tokyo's Mingeikan, or Japan Folk Crafts Museum. Our spoon was one of a handful that were similar but different – not just useful but unique, and without the flawless regularity of a machine-made object. The museum's shop was no ordinary gift store; it contained a meticulously curated collection of handmade objects by present-day Japanese makers, including ceramics, glass, paper and metalware.

The Japanese concept of finding beauty in the imperfect and embracing the humble is called *wabi-sabi*. It is not a decorating style, but a whole worldview. Walking through Mingeikan's galleries, *wabi-sabi* was abundantly present, in the simple rustic shapes of early hagi ware glazed pottery or the highly tactile, pitted cast-iron kettles. These objects seemed to have a soul, not least because their little imperfections were the result of having been made by hand.

Returning to Japan to take photographs for this book, we found that *wabi-sabi* was alive and well in many Japanese homes; the frayed, the weathered and the worn are embraced, and ordinary, practical objects are given elevated status by being displayed in a measured way. Widening our search, we uncovered homeowners all over the world who appreciate the imperfect. They have created inspiring spaces that are individual, yet share an understanding that battered, scuffed, peeling and even broken objects are not just beautiful, but preferable to pristine ones, because they bring a place to life and make it feel homely and personal.

INTRODUCTION

Each chapter of this book – textiles, texture, colour, handmade, collections – expand upon an element of the *wabi-sabi* home. They consider ways to incorporate these features into your own space, and focus more closely on a single home that encapsulates these ideas. We hope that they will inspire you to see the beauty in *wabi-sabi*.

WABI-SABI PHILOSOPHY

Austerity, asymmetry, modesty and simplicity: these are some of the characteristics of *wabi-sabi*, a philosophy embedded in Japanese Zen Buddhism and culture. This aesthetic is sometimes described as one of beauty that is 'imperfect, impermanent, and incomplete'. Our book embodies this belief and sets out to show you how to achieve it in your home.

Flawlessness is to be admired in some quarters, but it is hard to justify in the home. From an aesthetic point of view, rigid symmetry and uniform texture and colours do little to stimulate the eye, or the imagination, and from a practical perspective, even the most pristine house will soon be subject to the ravages of daily life.

We believe in a looser, more relaxed approach. We're not advocating that you forget about housework or let your possessions pile up unhindered, but that you surround yourself with everyday, irregular things that you love to look at. Indeed, you should welcome them in, as a way to achieve a sense of true homeliness.

The *wabi-sabi* approach might mean finding more spontaneous ways to display art and handcrafted pieces; being more flexible will enable you to easily change things around you if you tire of them. It might entail patching and mending textiles rather than throwing them away. Integrity is easier to achieve when you choose handmade objects over machine-made ones, especially humbler items that you touch every day, like glasses and tableware, mixing and matching them to create a pleasing contrast.

When it comes to the backdrop for your objects, a calm, neutral setting will make things stand out. However, if you are lucky enough to live in an older home where surfaces have been built up over successive decades, you may well have a rich treasure trove of uneven walls, doors and other features just waiting to be uncovered. Try peeling back the layers instead of covering them up to add a vital textural element to the home that speaks of its honesty.

ORDINARY IRREGULARITY
Surround yourself with things you love to look at, no matter how ordinary or irregular they might be. In the dining room of our home on the Welsh borders (opposite), chalky white walls, flagstone floors and a scuffed canteen table with a black linoleum top provide a stable, unchanging backdrop that allows us to experiment with new ways to display.

We all delight in the unexpected, and displaying items for their patina, their silhouette or simply their craftsmanship can make you see them in a new light. Objects that are broken, incomplete or obsolete may have lost their original function, but they can still be displayed as beautiful things in their own right or, better still, given a new life. Reusing things will not only challenge your creative skills, but makes for a thrifty approach too. And you can often find that scuffed, peeling and battered objects have a natural affinity with one another, helping to create a sense of harmony with less effort.

OUT IN THE OPEN
Dispense with drawers and cupboards (opposite and above left) and keep your treasures out on display. In our home, we use a galvanized metal industrial rail attached to an old French monastery bench in lieu of a wardrobe (above left). A similar rail divides the space in our studio, where canvas panels act as walls (below).

Nature also has its part to play in the *wabi-sabi* home, and not just in the introduction of natural materials, such as coarse-grained timbers or hand-woven textiles. Plants and flowers are the epitome of effortless imperfection, especially cut flowers, which seem to droop and decay just as beautifully as they once lived. The Victorian art critic John Ruskin believed that embracing the imperfect puts us more in harmony with a natural world that is changing, growing and dying all the time : 'Nothing that lives is rigidly perfect; part of it is decaying, part nascent,' he wrote, concluding that 'to banish imperfection is to destroy expression, to check exertion, to paralyse vitality'. Ruskin's words carry even more weight today, because we need an antidote to our fast, polished, high-tech world. *Wabi-sabi* is that salve, and home is the place to start.

CREASED

Creased, crumpled, patched, frayed and wrinkled: there lies the beauty in old cloth. Once, on a trip to Tokyo, we were taken to see an incredible museum containing a collection of work clothes and textiles referred to as *boro*, meaning continually mended and patched. The collection of 30,000 pieces was amassed over many years by Chuzaburo Tanaka and is now a national treasure. The clothes were once worn by the peasant farming communities of the snowy northern region of Japan and were handed down from generation to generation. We were encouraged to try them on, and this we found very strange, as normally anything so old and fragile would be kept behind glass and firmly out of reach. This experience had such a profound impact on us that on our return it became one of the founding principles of the *wabi-sabi* home – *boro* being the antithesis of modern consumer culture as the fabric reflects the beauty of wear and use. Since then, we actively seek out old fabrics with repairs and patching, and get incredibly excited by them and the ways in which we can incorporate them into the home. Thick Hungarian linen cart covers can be cut up to make duvet covers, and French linen tea/dish towels sewn together to make pillowcases. The list is endless – all you need is some imagination and basic sewing skills, and off you go.

{preloved & faded}

VINTAGE

Part of the appeal of vintage textiles is their rarity; easily degraded by the sun or worn away by use, many fabrics do not last more than a lifetime. It makes the survivors all the more special. Textiles span class, geography and culture – everyone needs to be clothed and kept warm – and provide fascinating insights into everyday life. The *wabi-sabi* philosophy believes that the humblest objects are the most evocative, like patched and faded workwear that speaks of hardship and thrift in every fold. Old fabrics are rarely regular, either in their initial weaving or their subsequent stitching together, which gives them a subtle sense of imperfection. But they also age in wonderful ways: falling into rags, fading to soft colours and letting whatever is underneath – horsehair, wool batting – burst through. So they are doubly imperfect, and all the more beautiful for it.

TEXTILES AGE IN WONDERFUL WAYS: FALLING TO RAGS, FADING TO SOFT COLOURS.

MADE FOR SHADE
These indigo-dyed parasols in linen
and cotton were used by French
shepherds at the turn of the last
century to keep off the sun. All
slightly different in size and in
the design of their wooden handles,
they look sculptural as an informal
collection of objects, the deep folds
of fabric bringing out their depth
of colour. Once opened up, the
umbrellas reveal an almost tie-dyed
effect, with streaks of darker blue
created by selective fading.

LAYERS OF HISTORY

Imperfection is sometimes seen as a virtue at the production stage when it comes to textiles; this hanging (above left) would be a duller proposition if its pattern were regular. Layering fabrics can make for rich and exotic interiors, whether they are more everyday objects, such as a coat-stand of Indian bags (above right), or an inviting place to rest (opposite). The passage of time can do wonderful things to fragile fabrics, like this frayed and patched upholstery, bulging with escaping horsehair (right).

CAREFREE REPAIRS

Antique furniture can sometimes be a little stand-offish, so grand or so elegant that you don't want to touch or use it. But there's something very inviting about the buttoned sofa (this page) in Anna Phillips' Sussex home, in no small part because of the carefree way it's been repaired, with big patches of fabric stitched over any damage. It's not delicate, not attempting concealment – just honest.

SOFT LINENS

Anna's relaxed style has a lot to do with her choice of textiles (opposite). She favours washed linen over crisply ironed sheets, which are pleasingly crumpled and get softer to the touch with every wash. Unlined linen curtains in soft colours, embroidered pillowcases and unpretentious furniture all serve to emphasize her taste for the homely and handmade.

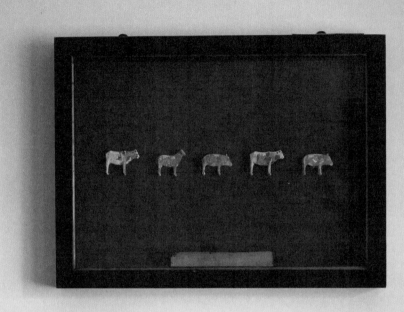

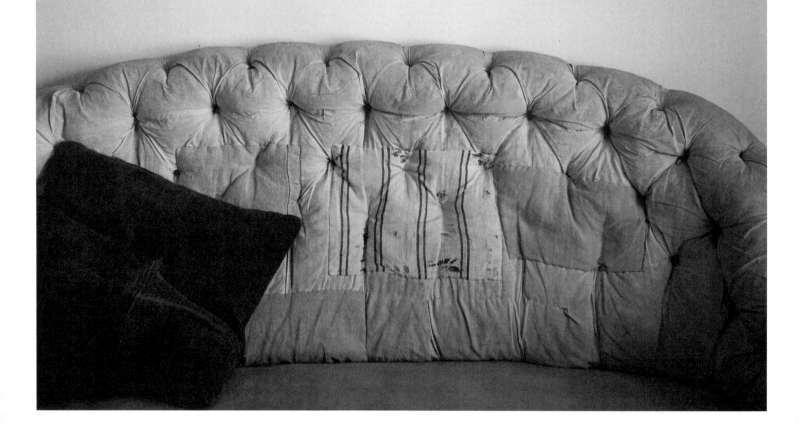

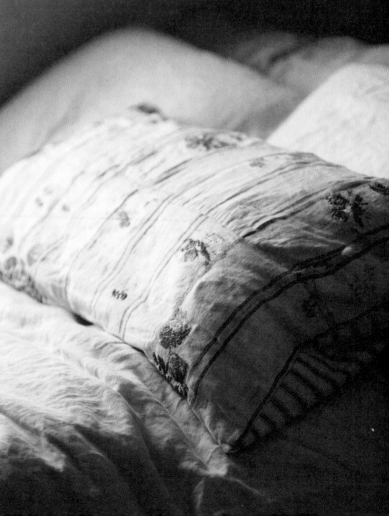

RECYCLED

'Make do and mend' existed as a philosophy for centuries before it was crystallized into a wartime slogan, simply because cloth was too precious to throw away. But beyond mending and patching what already exists, there's also creative mileage to be had from reinventing textiles as new objects for the home. It sometimes takes imagination to see potential, especially in things whose original purpose is not domestic, like industrial sacking, but these hard-wearing items often make the most durable and characterful homewares of all. Needless to say, it's also very thrifty, with a little going a long way – it doesn't take much fabric to make a cushion or lampshade, so small offcuts can often have a big impact.

TEXTILES WITH A TWIST
Industrial textiles such as grain or flour sacks make robust home textiles, with a little intrigue added by their graphic lettering. Two patched grain sacks fill up this bench (opposite), their darned sections at odds with the refined oak barley-twist carving on the arms. Just as rustic looking but much more delicate is Japanese *kaya* (mosquito net fabric, usually made from hemp), which has been stitched to make midge-proof window panels (this page).

IT SOMETIMES TAKES IMAGINATION TO SEE POTENTIAL, ESPECIALLY IN OBJECTS WHOSE ORIGINAL PURPOSE IS NOT DOMESTIC.

RAGS TO RICHES

Even the smallest scraps have the potential to turn into something special when they are used in quantity. Here (opposite, clockwise from top left), a patchwork of recycled sari fabric has been used to make a lampshade; wrapped fabric balls enliven an otherwise unused space on a staircase; plain wire coat-hangers turn into something much more charming when they're covered in wound strips of textiles; and frayed indigo cotton creates a tactile handle.

SUNNY DISPOSITION

Hummingly bright yellow walls make this bedroom a stimulating place in which to wake up. The sari lampshade adds to the vibrancy, but it's tempered by the plainness of the bedlinen and the pillowcase, which is made from a striped Hungarian linen grain sack.

SACKING FOR SEATING

Jute sacking stretches over the seat of this country wooden bench in our home (opposite and right); it's given a softer look with an arrangement of cushions in vegetable-dyed indigo from Ghana. The traditional resist-dyeing techniques that have been used to make the fabric produce some beautifully uneven results – star-like constellations against a night sky, or thick bands of scratched-out sections. Each piece is quite different, but unified by the glorious deep blue background.

THE TRADITIONAL RESIST-DYEING TECHNIQUES THAT HAVE BEEN USED TO MAKE THE FABRIC PRODUCE SOME BEAUTIFULLY UNEVEN RESULTS.

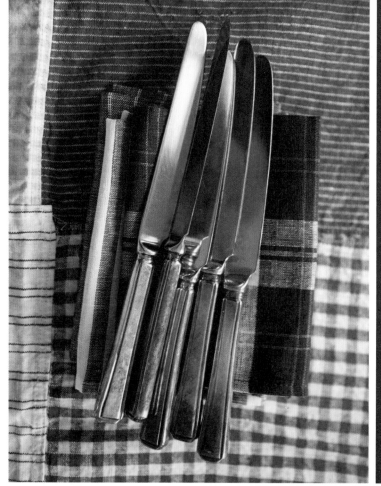

USEFUL FRAGMENTS

Wabi-sabi embraces asymmetry and economy and patchwork possesses both these qualities. Here (above left and above), kitchen towels from Yumiko Sekine's Fog Linen Work have been stitched together to screen off our spare bedroom in an open-plan space, which looks appealing when the light shines through it. Smaller scraps (left) have been used to make an equally attractive patchwork tablecloth.

FRAMING THE VIEW

We've employed the same idea of a patchwork curtain at home (opposite), with Fog Linen Work textiles hung at the window to create a light, diaphanous frame onto the world outside. They are deliberately mismatched, with the purple checked gingham holding the eye on both sides.

{everyday textiles}

SIMPLE

Some people love the crisp feel of ironed, starched bedlinen, the kind of sheets you find in five-star hotels. But washed and well-worn linen – the type that gets comfier with every wash, and looks better artfully rumpled rather than neatly ironed – is more appealing to anyone who is drawn to the *wabi-sabi* world view. We believe you should always invest the most in the objects that get daily use. Bedlinen is high up that list, not just because you will get everyday pleasure from it but because it will last longer; the same goes for towels and kitchen towels/dish cloths. What's more, if you stick to white you'll never have to worry about what matches what – you can enliven everyday textiles with a roster of more exciting throws, blankets and cushions that can alter the mood.

CRUMPLED LINEN

A typhoon had just passed through when we visited this serene apartment, belonging to floral artist and stylist Noriko Inomoto, in the heart of bustling Tokyo. It made the tranquil linen-clad bedroom (opposite) seem like a calm haven after the storm. Noriko has devised a clever but simple method of hanging her curtains (this page). She generously folds the linen over, then threads lengths of fine jute string through the fabric at even intervals, knotting them over a metal pole.

TEXTILE GALLERY
The simple metal frame bedhead (this page) acts as a sort of informal gallery for whatever textiles have caught our eye; here, it's draped in Ghanaian tie-dyed indigo throws, hanging at different lengths to make the display asymmetrical. The off-white wall and natural bedlinen mean that whatever we put here always stands out.

THE INDIGO PLANT HAS BEEN USED FOR CENTURIES TO DYE UTILITARIAN FABRICS.

SHADES OF HARMONY

One of the pleasures of living with textiles is making them work together, their different weights, colours, patterns and textures creating a harmonious mix. Natural materials such as cottons and linens, dyed in subtle organic shades taken from nature, will nearly always look great together. Above (clockwise from top left), Fog Linen Work's Lithuanian-made kitchen cloths work well alone, but their many different designs are created to be mixed and matched; stacked linens in Tokyo store Starnet, which specializes in handmade crafts; textural interplay between a fringed throw and the crumpled sheet beneath it; more Starnet linens – thanks to the hand-dyeing process, no two colours, from raspberry pink to mushroom grey, are repeated; Fog Linen Work's linens, showing the lovely uneven weave that stands out when held up to the light; a detail of our patchwork curtain of Fog Linen Work fabrics.

HISTORICAL THREAD

Fog Linen Work's bedlinen (opposite) is made in Lithuania, and follows the same ethos of simple functionality as its kitchen textiles. Lithuania has been growing flax and making linen since the Middle Ages, so these crumpled white sheets in Ryuji Mitani's home have a prestigious heritage. Yumiko Sekine's talent has been to harness the quality of the raw material and use it to make products for a wider audience.

INFORMAL WELCOME

Loose cushions can lend grander pieces of furniture, such as the stripped-down Chesterfield in our home (this page), a welcoming informality. The unpretentious nature of the textiles themselves helps reinforce this – a mix of smart, classic ticking and the more unusual ombré dip-dyed cushion along the backrest.

A PRODUCT OF NATURE

With its simple linen curtain and scuffed timber stool, the changing room at Starnet in Tokyo (this page) is a cut above the average retail experience. The light perfectly captures the unique qualities of linen: soft, lightly textured and, in its undyed state, an obvious product of nature.

LIVING CONTRASTS

The patinated industrial floor lights and tin trunk are in contrast to our Baileys Loft Sofa at home (opposite). It is covered in naturally dyed linen, which gives a relaxed look that gets better with age.

MATERIAL WORLD

Antiques dealer Katharine Pole specializes in French textiles, a fact that is very clear on a visit to her North London home, which is packed with her fabric finds. She and her husband have only lived here for a couple of years, but it doesn't seem that way – their home looks more like it has evolved over decades. Katharine says she was sold on the place the moment she saw the peeling wallpaper upstairs, which was half stripped away to reveal mottled plaster beneath. The abundance of textiles, many of them patched and frayed, makes a significant contribution to the feeling of a well-lived-in home, adding warmth, colour, pattern and texture all in one go.

CURATED CLOTH

Ripped and faded fabrics adorn Katharine's home. The stitched circles (above left) are buffing discs once used for mechanical polishing in a workshop; textile-covered boxes in faded hues are stacked with books (above right). The workroom-cum-showroom (opposite) is home to an 18th-century French four-poster, its silk linen canopy ravaged by age.

PILED HIGH
Textiles, mostly sourced from France, are stacked up on an old patisserie stand (opposite). The oil-on-canvas floral artwork tucked behind it is a fragment of what would have been a much larger wall covering.

BLUE HUES
The fabric storage boxes (right) were once used to hold bills and papers belonging to Katharine's father-in-law; now she keeps scraps of fabric inside. The hatbox and bonnet, both in a washed-out blue, date from the early 19th century, and the same shades are picked out in the portrait and dried flowers.

The stacked quilts that Katharine displays at home (mostly French, but a few English) have a gently repetitive palette, with dusky pink, off-white and indigo as the recurring theme. Indigo is one of her passions; as a small girl, her family lived in northern Nigeria, and she can remember the Tuareg guards of their living compound, who would sit around drinking mint tea, wearing magnificent indigo turbans. Now, she collects and sells French *biaude* clothing that was once rustic workwear. Originally darkest blue, these smocks and shop-coats have faded in a poetic way that reminds one of endless days of hard graft in the sun, and the endless hand-washing that must have followed.

A patched-up indigo linen skirt on a mannequin is one of Katharine's most treasured pieces. It typifies her approach to display, singling out some of the most humble and imperfect items in her collection for special scrutiny. And while the upstairs showroom-cum-

bedroom is rich in layers of colour and texture, downstairs there is an air of calm. White walls and natural floorboards set off a few special items of furniture, many given an unexpected twist: a 19th-century chair has been reupholstered in 1980s denim, but with a brash red stripe of antique wool and linen at the back. Other chairs are left *déshabillé*, their horsehair stuffing peeking out.

Fabric finds its way into unexpected places, like a glass bottle lampstand, which is stitched up in a mummy-like wrapping of 19th-century toile, or the jars of antique scraps, leftovers from Katharine's cushion- and lampshade-making. The fact that she cannot bear to throw anything away, no matter how small or frayed, is testament to her passion for textiles, but these scraps are also a little window into a time when textiles were constantly stitched, darned, patched and otherwise reinvented out of sheer necessity.

INGENIOUS USES

This house uses textiles in
unusual and creative ways.
The sofa and antique chair have
been reupholstered in 1970s
denim, but Katharine has put
a bold stripe of 19th-century
fabric on the back of the chair
because she knew that it would
be seen from the other end of
the room (this page). A pair
of 18th-century doors, covered
in layers of old wallpaper,
have been rebuilt as storage
cupboards (opposite left).
French and English linens fill
an open shelving unit, while
indigo-dyed shepherds' parasols
lean against it (opposite right).

Q&A

Perfect or imperfect? Perfect imperfection.

Is there anything in your home you would consider 'perfectly imperfect'? The cupboard in the kitchen, made from a pair of 18th-century doors. It's covered in peeling layers of 19th-century block-printed wallpaper: a chalky pale floral, a geometric pattern and a peep of blue-and-white ticking stripe. With an old iron latch and a perfect, flaky, French grey-painted base, it is imperfect perfection created by time (and a bit of help from an ingenious carpenter).

What's the biggest talking point in your home when people visit? The 18th-century four-poster bed in my workroom/showroom. The awning and hanging, all a little tattered, are of a faded heavy red-and-beige-striped linen and silk textile, and the double scallops are edged in the palest of yellow silk. The bed is piled high with quilts and cushions (and often a sleeping Jack Russell terrier and a cat), and takes pride of place in the room with a simple presence that pleases the eye.

What are you working on now?
A collection of lampshades in antique textiles.

Likes: Indigo blues. The paintings of Velázquez, Ingres and Félix Vallotton. Darns and patches. The films of Visconti. Old roses and topiary. Family life. An antique piece of furniture *dans son jus*. A pile of Provençal quilts. An emptying beach at the end of a summer's day.

Dislikes: Predictability.

Worn objects have a story to tell. They can almost seem alive with their sense of the past, especially if they carry traces of human intervention – the painted chair worn down to smooth wood where a back has rested against it for decades, or the antique jacket that still bears the ghostly definition of its former wearer. Your imagination can float away on ideas of who touched them, when and why. You may find that you can't resist touching them yourself. Going even deeper, you might find that it gives you a sense of your own mortality.

The *wabi-sabi* philosophy is that scuffed, torn and weathered belongings are beautiful in their own right. Peeling paintwork can produce unexpectedly lovely layers of colour, while old textiles possess a papery delicacy that their modern counterparts can't match. These objects are also unique: no one else will have a worn-out chair patched up in quite the same way as yours; no one else's tin bucket for firewood will have exactly the same dents and bumps as yours. Industrial objects and materials often have interesting patination because they were never intended to remain pristine, nor were they treated with kid gloves in their working life.

{texture}

SCUFFED

Tactility is an underrated quality, but it is very important. It introduces the added dimension that gives a home a soul, stimulating two senses at once: the eye, as it takes in the mix of hard and soft, rough and smooth; and the hand, when surfaces prove too tempting not to touch. Contrast is good – think about mixing cool-feeling concrete with warm wool, or placing reflective materials, such as glass or glazed ceramics, next to matt ones, like tarnished metal or unpolished wood. Equally, though, you should treat texture as you might colour; a riot of different shades is jarring, and a large number of different surfaces can also feel like too much.

ROUGH FINISHES ARE ALSO DYNAMIC, CREATING A MOBILE PLAY OF SHADOWS ACROSS THEIR SURFACE AS THE DAY WEARS ON.

{flaking plaster, rough finishes}

EXPOSED

Old houses are often crooked, generally due to many decades of slight movement. Cracks appear in walls and ceilings, and floors heave, groan and finally settle, all adding to the overall wonkiness. They are also uneven in texture, displaying their age by way of peeling paint and scuffed plasterwork. Our home on the Welsh borders, pictured here, was built of local stone and finished with lime plaster, which incorporated horsehair to hold everything together. These uneven surfaces are interesting and do not shout out or compete with the other objects in the room. They contrast well with other surfaces, such as the cast-iron stove and the decorative carved door jamb from India, now a mantelpiece. Rough finishes are also dynamic, creating a mobile play of shadows across their surface as the day wears on.

WHITE SWAN FEATHERS ARE SIMPLY TAPED TO THE WALL,
THEIR DOWNY ENDS QUIVERING WITH MOVEMENT.

ANIMAL INSTINCTS

Introducing organic materials
is an easy way to temper some
of the hard surfaces in a home.
An organically cured sheepskin
fills a Bertoia chair by the
fire (this page), its deep pile
offering an inviting place to
sit, and the lush brown shade
on its outer edge picking up
on the mellow aged timber
of the mantel. The white swan
feathers (opposite) are simply
taped to the wall, their downy
ends quivering with movement.

INDUSTRIOUS BEHAVIOUR

This corner of our home (opposite) really shows off the character of the unfinished plaster in that indistinguishable shade of grey-pink, mottled and blotched over time. An American tin ceiling tile propped against the wall is used as a moodboard, its dull metallic glow matched by the steel desk and chairs.

STANDING TALL

The chalky walls are mostly left unadorned – it's easier to move things around when objects are placed on the floor or on tables, like the numbered bus blind (above), which stands next to a Carl Zeiss tripod lamp with a gleaming mirrored shade. Fragments of gilded shop signs (above left) give that same glimmer against the matt walls. We've hung African shell necklaces on the chunky hooks next to the soot-blackened fireplace (left), with low Ethiopian stools positioned either side.

53

CRATE STORAGE

We have been using redundant crates for years. This is our latest reincarnation (left): a freestanding stacked system, with metal deed boxes sandwiched in between, creating an even rhythm of different textures, balanced by one of our tripod lamps with a brioche tin shade and an old inspection lamp.

WONDER WALLS

Reveal the history of your home by peeling back layers of wallpaper and paint (opposite). Like counting the rings of a tree, you can almost work out the age of a house from the decorating trends or disasters of the time. Be prepared for surprises.

{wood meets metal}

AGED

Wabi-sabi values the beauty that comes with age and decay. Both wood and metal take on wonderful qualities as they get older, with wood maturing to deep, dark hues or lightening to warm, creamy shades (and everything in between), and metal oxidizing to complex and sometimes surprisingly bright colours – rust red or sea-green verdigris. Putting the two side by side gives the best of both worlds, where natural meets man-made. We also like to mix highly crafted wooden items with much more functional industrial furniture, so that delicate, skilled workmanship can be played off against sturdy, robust functionality.

DELICATELY BALANCED
A row of vertically stacked pieces of wood —
decorative architectural carvings and a salvaged
shop sign — demonstrates the rich palette of tones
and textures of aged timber (opposite). Compare
the delicacy of the carving with the utilitarian
charms of the rusty metal table. In our bedroom
(this page), salvaged items such as upturned dolly
tubs and stripped Hungarian wooden doors make
bedside tables and a headboard respectively.

BURIED TREASURE

Wood's ability to be reworked and remade into something new makes it highly sustainable. Small pieces of driftwood have been embedded into a concrete floor (above), offering an attractive patchwork of different surfaces. More driftwood, along with salvaged wire and steel, forms the stair balustrade and handrail.

PICKING OUT THE GRAIN

Worn away by the sea, driftwood is blessed with a silky smoothness that makes it hard not to touch, so it's perfect for handles. Mismatched driftwood handles set at different angles turn a chest of drawers in Noriko Inomoto's Tokyo apartment (above right and opposite) into a focal point; the deep grain on the drawer fronts is accentuated by the sun-bleached wood.

SLEIGH BEDS

In Anna Phillips' Sussex home, the children's beds (right) are made from ware boards, once used in Staffordshire potteries for carrying ceramics. These boards make versatile additions to the home – Anna has also used them for her kitchen shelving – and their years of use imbue them with a characterful mellowness.

MAKESHIFT PANELLING

We've used pottery ware boards in our home like
impromptu panelling (left), stacking them up together
and bookending them with American tin ceiling tiles;
some of the boards bear a pattern of rings where the
pottery once stood. The objects in front have been
chosen for their similar muted colours and also their
interesting textures, such as the scored lines on an
old leather football and the rough coils of a pile of
rope. Paint-spattered boards provide the backdrop for
a child's wheelbarrow, used as storage, and a vintage
shop sign that reads 'Parsons Trunks' (above).

A RECLAIMED KITCHEN
In Anna Phillips' smoky grey kitchen (this page), the cupboards are made from weathered fruit crates, disbanded, cut up and reassembled to make doors and drawers – a modern take on marquetry panels. Ware board shelving (opposite) holds her collection of stoneware.

DRIFTWOOD EYRIE

Offcuts of driftwood are used to magical effect in cult Japanese denim store Okura, to make this overhead shack that, in its sculptural idiosyncrasy, looks almost like a work of art in a gallery.

WEATHERED WOOD

Opposite, clockwise from top left: wood always carries its history so well, like these weathered and worn boards in Masakazu Yonehara's Tokyo store Ensyu; look closer and you will see that tiny letterpress blocks and moss have been pushed carefully into the gaps between these floorboards; a detail of the extraordinary 400-year-old Nuristani house that now sits in Pip Rau's North London home – the reflective dots glinting in the carved fruitwood panels are mica; more of the moss- and letterpress-filled floor, showing the wonderful graining and dark knots of the boards themselves.

UNPOLISHED

Stripping something back to its natural state lets you see its materials for what they are. Boiled down to the essentials, powdery brickwork, bleached wood and uncoated paper have an honest simplicity that seems to act like a blanket of calm over a home. Keeping it simple like this makes it easy to mix and match objects in lots of different materials or shapes because they all have that rawness about them to tie everything together. We love incorporating metal, but when it's polished to a high shine, we only ever use it in small doses, where it serves to underscore the mix of matt textures everywhere else. Metal that's been clouded by time, on the other hand, is sublime; it has a certain mysteriousness and looks wonderful under low, flickering light. So instead of breaking out the silver polish, light some candles and relax instead!

POWDERY, BRICKWORK, BLEACHED WOOD AND UNCOATED PAPER HAVE AN HONEST SIMPLICITY THAT SEEMS TO ACT LIKE A BLANKET OF CALM OVER A HOME.

PAST GLORIES

With most of the mercury mirror glass long gone from this dull ormolu frame (above), many people would have rejected it as being beyond saving. Luckily, its owner, Anna Phillips, spotted its potential and has used the empty rebate to house old photographs. Anna has also painstakingly relined the inside of an old lamp with silk remnants (above left and opposite). The surreal and unexpected definitely have a place in the imperfect home: how about this caged light fitting (far left), with a tap 'dripping' a lightbulb, or a jointed table lamp (left) wall-mounted on an old lavatory seat?

IN THE DETAIL

Opposite, clockwise from top left: we like the fact that Japanese denim store Okura even paint their bins indigo; nature has started to make a claim on this vintage bicycle – the black and purple leaves and buds have a remarkably similar tone to the rusted frame; intriguing surface pattern can be found in unexpected places – this whitewashed window has begun to be scratched away and looks like tiny organisms under a microscope. Another natural intervention (above left), a twine-like branch of dark berries casually rests around a bell-shaped light; deed boxes make excellent storage (above), placed haphazardly on top of one another to maximize impact.

BATHED IN TEXTURE

Reclaimed skirting/base boards wrap around the bathtub in our bathroom (above); the 'sink or swim' sign is made up from old letterpress characters. Grouping together objects of the same material but that had a very different original purpose can make you look twice. The array of storage above the sink (opposite), for example, consists of baking trays and deed boxes, alongside more conventional mirrored cabinets.

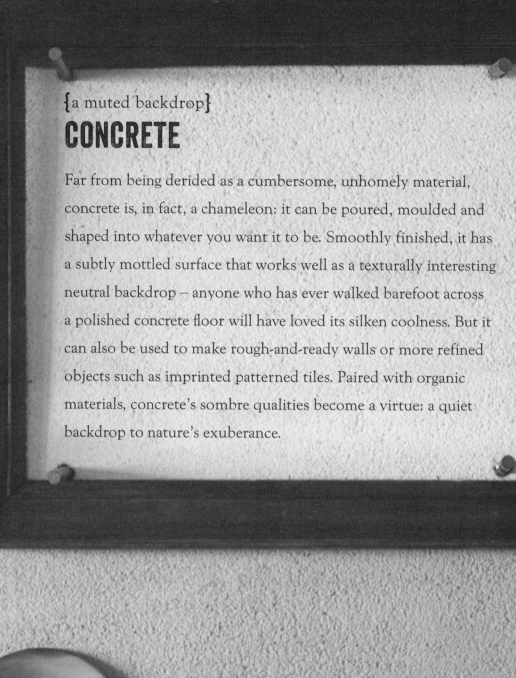

{a muted backdrop}

CONCRETE

Far from being derided as a cumbersome, unhomely material, concrete is, in fact, a chameleon: it can be poured, moulded and shaped into whatever you want it to be. Smoothly finished, it has a subtly mottled surface that works well as a texturally interesting neutral backdrop – anyone who has ever walked barefoot across a polished concrete floor will have loved its silken coolness. But it can also be used to make rough-and-ready walls or more refined objects such as imprinted patterned tiles. Paired with organic materials, concrete's sombre qualities become a virtue: a quiet backdrop to nature's exuberance.

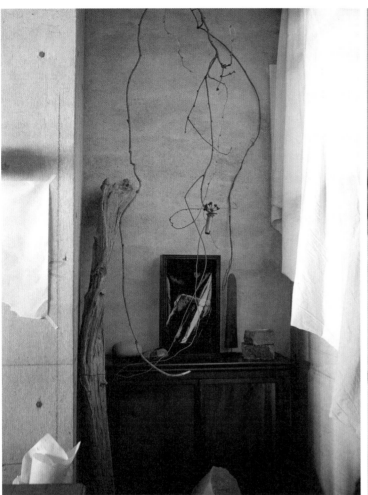

STILL LIFE

Opposite, clockwise from top left:
an atmospheric still life of vessels at
Kazuto Kobayashi's Outbound store
in Tokyo; an oak bread board from
France, propped up on the concrete
shelf in our kitchen; the lustre of these
glazed ceramics makes them stand
out against their concrete background;
broken pottery has been pushed into
the concrete floor, with some pieces
having come loose, leaving intriguing
indents behind.

TEXTURAL TEAMWORK

Clockwise from above: a tangle of vine
silhouetted against a concrete wall at
Kobayashi's Outbound store; Costanza
Algranti's unique kitchen units have two
contrasting metal finishes: stainless steel
for the workstops, and a patchwork of
zinc panels for the sides.

SOFT TOUCH

Aged timber has the effect of softening harder
industrial surfaces such as steel and concrete.
A Tokyo kitchen at Starnet (this page) makes up
for lack of space with a playful use of reclaimed
planks to create a 'striped' island unit. At
eclectic Tokyo store Outbound, wooden crates
and shelves, repurposed as storage, sit against
a concrete wall (opposite). Filled with wooden
and ceramic objects, they have been masterfully
arranged to entice people to look closer.

THE ALCHEMIST

Designer Costanza Algranti loves to give new life to discarded objects. The furniture that she creates from wood, zinc and copper is recycled from materials hauled from landfill sites, and a large part of their appeal is their wonderful patination, as well as their textural quality. Costanza lives in Milan's Isola district, in an apartment block that was once a neighbourhood *centro sociale*, the equivalent of a cultural community centre. Her aim was to furnish the place entirely with her own creations, and in doing so she has created a home that is uniquely inventive, showing just what is possible when a fertile imagination is paired with making skills.

TACTILE KITCHEN

The open-plan kitchen (opposite) contrasts a smooth concrete floor and stainless-steel work surface with Costanza's rougher, handmade furniture. The visible rivets of the table (above right) and curled wire of the lampshade (above left) remain on show, creating a sense of simplicity that contrasts with their complex patination.

MULTI-TEXTURED
The kitchen is Costanza's favourite room because of the soft light that enters it early in the morning. Taking a multi-textured approach to design can turn your home into a dynamic environment that is forever changing as the light moves round during the day, casting subtle shadows.

Taken on shape alone, Costanza's furniture veers towards the sturdy and industrial, but the various textures playing over their surfaces make the pieces seem gentler and more domestic. The patchwork of galvanized zinc wrapped around the kitchen units is a case in point. With its visible riveting and uncompromisingly boxy shape, it is firmly industrial, but look closer at the texture and it is lovely: a mélange of greys and browns as delicate as silver-birch bark. The inclusion of so much rough timber – a failsafe material for providing textural interest – is vital, as it acts as a foil for the harder concrete and steel. You can sense the lightness of the wood, just as you can the heaviness of the copper and zinc.

Here, texture is not just about something you can feel when you run your hands over an object; it provides something for the eye, too. Choosing materials that slowly develop layers of different colour, from scuffed painted chairs to patinated copper, gives a subtle sense of the passing of time. There is not much bright colour used in this home – it doesn't need it, given that there is so much else to take in – but what colour there is has a mineral palette that chimes well with the wood and concrete. Particularly spectacular is the oxidized copper, its iridescent sheen as beautiful as a beetle's wing – proof that a chemical process can produce just as magnificent a sight as nature.

ASYMMETRY

All the furniture is made from reclaimed wood, including the cabinets in the two bathrooms (above left and right), the kitchen storage, whose chunky wooden casing contrasts with the copper doors (far right), and the bed (opposite), whose headboard was a sign on a Livorno fishing boat (it reads, 'Caution, moving propellers'). There's a pleasing sense of asymmetry about the storage that wraps itself up and over the headboard, as well as some unexpected touches, like the recycled boards sunk into the floor (right), acting as a kind of wooden rug, breaking up the expanse of concrete.

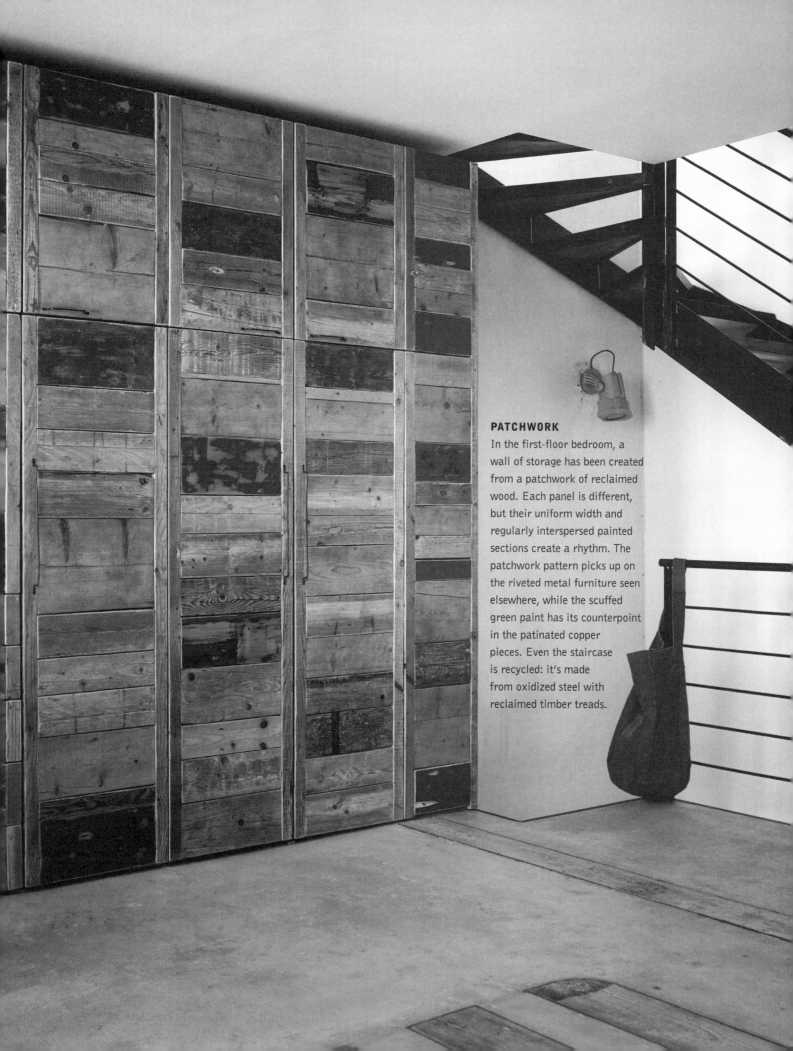

PATCHWORK

In the first-floor bedroom, a wall of storage has been created from a patchwork of reclaimed wood. Each panel is different, but their uniform width and regularly interspersed painted sections create a rhythm. The patchwork pattern picks up on the riveted metal furniture seen elsewhere, while the scuffed green paint has its counterpoint in the patinated copper pieces. Even the staircase is recycled: it's made from oxidized steel with reclaimed timber treads.

Perfect or imperfect? Imperfect.

Is there anything in your home you would consider 'perfectly imperfect'? Everything, because all my works are based on the 'praise of imperfection'. The imperfection of all my creations is what gives them their added value. With my work, I try as much as possible to use the material as I found it, giving it a new chance and a new life.

Do you have a favourite object in your house? What is it, and where did it come from?
The copper cupboard in the living room. I created it from a big copper gutter found in a landfill. I usually use copper, zinc, steel and wood; they work well together because they have different colours and a different weight and structure.

How would you spend the ideal day at home?
Feeling at ease. Feeling comfortable doing the things that I like most: reading, cooking, listening to music and being with my friends. I love to open my house to my friends and share my creations with them.

Likes: The sea. Running.

What are you reading at the moment?
Haruki Murakami's *Kafka on the Shore*.

What music do you enjoy listening to?
Pat Metheny.

What are you working on now? I'm working on a big, big kitchen for a country house. And I'm very happy with it.

Wabi-sabi appreciates the natural world, and nature rarely puts a foot wrong when it comes to colour, creating harmony even with hues from opposite ends of the spectrum. Natural materials, and plant- and mineral-derived colours, make a wonderful starting point when introducing colour to your home. Everything will have an affinity, from driftwood that's bleached palest cream, to the hot reds of textiles dyed with madder root, to a bowlful of knobbly Amalfi lemons.

Naturally derived colours also sit well with the hues found in industrial materials, such as dark green or amber glass, or the flaming russet of rusty iron. Introduce the smallest lick of something new and bright for fun, and that should be all you need. It usually works best to keep the background neutral – you're less likely to get bored of it, and it will better show off your furniture and objects – and the definition of 'neutral' is surprisingly broad. Conker brown, inky blue-black, duck egg blue and palest concrete grey are all colours that chime with one other and are easy to live with.

Aged objects, be they natural or man-made, are never a uniform colour. Over the decades, as their paint peels or they fade in the sun, they take on multiple tones. The added textural dimension of patinated colour is so much more interesting than a single flat shade. You can play around with patination and shading on a larger scale, by decorating a wall with large blocks of many similar tones of one colour, for example, or by using mineral-based paints like clay paints or limewash, which can produce pleasingly uneven results. And instead of worrying about the scuffs and marks that may come with these ultra-matt finishes, embrace them as part of a natural ageing process that has its own beauty. They will perfectly match the rest of your *wabi-sabi* home.

{colour}

SHADED

{washed-out dip-dyed indigo}

INKY HUES

Natural dyes are often mistakenly associated with dull and muted shades, but these images are enough to dispel that. Plant-derived indigo is a rich, saturated blue, so strong that it can turn its surroundings to an inky haze. Natural indigo is one of the earliest dyes ever used; India, Japan and West Africa all have a tradition of incorporating it into clothing and other textiles, with the West following suit once trading routes with these regions became established. The colour has strong links with practical fabrics, and workwear in particular, being durable and able to hide dirt. Surviving work clothes such as French *biaude* smocks and jackets are cheerfully weathered and faded, often patched up to preserve them. They make unusual objects for display in any home, as do modern indigo textiles, from tie-dyed throws to simple kitchen cloths.

COLOUR CONTRAST

What unites these images is the rich, saturated blue of
indigo dye. The colour that permeates the cloth is so strong
that it has the ability to turn its surroundings to an inky
blue haze. These simple curtains and linen patchwork
tablecloth (opposite left and right) almost vibrate with
saturated colour, as do the tie-dyed African scarves draped
majestically over the wall above the stairs at Japanese
denim store Okura (this page).

KIND OF BLUE
These stairs in Japanese denim store Okura have been covered in thick denim that has been glued to the concrete steps, radiating colour onto the wall (opposite, clockwise from top left); a resist-dyed curtain filters the light to a wash of palest blue; one of textile dealer Pip Rau's most treasured pieces is a Japanese *boro* jacket, made from offcuts artlessly stitched together; an antique Persian tile, which now sits in Pip Rau's kitchen, has retained its electric colour down the years.

SUBTLE SHADES
Clockwise from above: two-tone thread placed on top of a stack of indigo textiles, each one a subtly different shade; tie-dyed fabric gives a striking watercolour effect; simple clothing by Yumiko Sekine, sparsely hung on a steel and mesh hanging rail.

THE WORKING WARDROBE
Fog Linen Work's simply cut clothing (opposite) finds a perfect partner in indigo, which has a long association with humble garments. In this case, the colour is part of a wider message about the clothes' unpretentious nature. Still holding its inky colour, Mark's much-loved French jacket (this page) makes it easy to see why indigo was chosen for workwear – not only was the dye very durable, but it didn't show the dirt at a time when clothes were not washed regularly.

A KIND OF NEUTRAL

Despite its rich shade, indigo can qualify as a kind of neutral, making a subtle statement that isn't overpowering. Our Baileys Loft Corner Sofa is covered in thick blue Belgian linen, complemented with an indigo-dyed rag rug. The sofa is backed with mellow, heavily stained ware boards.

{intense, bright colour, pop accents}

VIBRANT

Strong colour can provoke strong reactions, and what is stimulating and uplifting to one person can be unsettling to another. This is one reason why it is easier to keep the backdrop of your home neutral, but a little risk taking can also be a wonderful thing. Bright colour often feels right when it is historical – like the chalky yellow ochre distemper on the walls in our house, seen here. It can also be exciting when multiple shades of the same colour are played off one another – not a conventional decorating idea, but one that results in a sort of enveloping hum of hue. Vibrant colour is also often employed as an essential, eye-catching full stop, from a single blowsy flower to an industrial lamp in fire engine red.

BRIGHT COLOUR CAN BE EXCITING WHEN SHADES OF THE SAME COLOUR PLAY OFF ONE ANOTHER – NOT A CONVENTIONAL DECORATING IDEA.

EXOTIC PALETTE
Building a room around similar tones of a single colour can have a dynamic, energizing effect. The 'hot' palette used here – saffron yellow, madder root orange – is reminiscent of an Indian festival, but the objects themselves betray some less exotic roots. The wall has been painted in differing tones of yellow, with the yellow jacket, an old theatre costume, providing some softness among the hard objects arranged on the wooden work bench (this page).

COLOUR CONTRADICTIONS

Creeping tongues of rust work their way over a panel of American tin painted a distinctive pea green (above, clockwise from top left); these bright balls of colour add an instant shot of cheeriness – we have them lined up on our stairs (see page 24); directly contrasting colours are the most eye-catching of all, such as this fluorescent stationery standing out against some purple tissue paper found in an old stationery shop in Paris; the soft, tufted edges of this pile of remnants make their bright colours blur together; the hand-crafted brass spoon contrasts with a heavily oxidized copper table made by Costanza Algranti; this door in our house has seen a number of bright colours over the years, so we selectively peeled back the layers to reveal all of them at the same time. Katharine Pole's remnant jars (opposite) are filled with all the fabric scraps that she can't bear to throw away.

GREAT AND SMALL
Bright colours don't need to be used in great
quantities to make an impact; our bathroom
(this page) uses fluorescent fishing floats to
add zing to the wood-and-white decoration.
At Japanese store Zakka (opposite), the red
metal panel is by Satoshi Nakata and acts as
the perfect foil for the three delicate teacups
by Natsu Hasegawa.

{soft, muted tones}
CHALKY

Historically, painted walls were made from products based on lime, clay or chalk – materials that were porous, to allow buildings to 'breathe'. They look different from modern paints, because they subtly blotch according to moisture levels, and also because they are very matt, gently diffusing the natural light and giving a room a softened appearance. Such finishes are finding favour again, in part because they are a better match for older houses and are more environmentally friendly, but also because of that elusive, subdued softness that seems to make such a difference. Aim for a home that runs the gamut between very matt surfaces – not just painted walls, but dust-rubbed chalkboard and dulled metal – right up to lustrous, high-shine ones, such as gilding, mica and mother-of-pearl, and you will have a full arsenal of visual variety to play around with.

MATT FINISHES ARE FINDING FAVOUR AGAIN, BECAUSE OF THAT ELUSIVE, SUBDUED SOFTNESS THAT SEEMS TO MAKE SUCH A DIFFERENCE.

HUSHED TONES

The luminous delicacy of pearl-handled
steel knives seems more pronounced
because of the scrubbed matt surface
on which they lie (opposite left). Pale
plastered walls are the background
for a diverse group of objects (opposite
right): a black tripod lamp, carved
Maori panels, with a hint of their
original red ochre stain, and some hazel
sticks. Chalky white walls (this page)
diffuse the natural light beautifully,
with a metal lamp and curly iron French
bed fitting in with the muted theme.

RESTFUL BLUES
Our cast-concrete shelf is the
backdrop for a serene still life of
handmade objects, gathered from
all over the world, in a harmonious
palette of soft blues and rich
browns. The bubble glass came
from Kabul; it sits alongside
celadon and French stoneware
and a Japanese raku bowl. The
advantages of this neutral setting
are that the coloured objects
immediately stand out – and we
can easily edit them, changing
them for something different when
a new colour catches our eye.

THE ADVANTAGES OF THIS NEUTRAL SETTING ARE THAT THE COLOURED
OBJECTS IMMEDIATELY STAND OUT – AND WE CAN CHANGE THEM FOR
SOMETHING DIFFERENT WHEN A NEW COLOUR CATCHES OUR EYE.

BEYOND THE PALE
White-on-white decorating
is easy, as long as you layer
up various different pale tones
and textures, to make a more
interesting whole, and add in
a few darker focal points, like
the indigo batik dressing gown
hung on the back of the door
(this page). Adrian Bannon's
ethereal Thistledown Coat has
an almost ghostly presence
above our deconstructed
Chesterfield (opposite).

FADE TO GREY
Inky blues and blue-greys again make their way into our home (opposite). The walls have been painted in large horizontal blocks of colour. Resembling a Pantone colour chart, they are separated by a thin line where the shelves used to be. A thickly striped blanket, slung over the old leather chair, picks up on the same shades. This simple unadorned fireplace fits neatly into the corner of Anna Phillip's kitchen (this page). Lime-plastered walls change and blotch according to moisture levels, allowing the house to breathe.

FADED

Absence of bright colour is not a reason for a home to be lifeless. A less-is-more attitude offers a chance to contemplate the innate qualities of natural materials and, more particularly, the craftsmanship and skill behind handmade objects. As long as there is a wider regard for mixing up texture, shape and tone, there should still be a wealth of visual interest. Try using objects with strong, dark silhouettes against pale walls (or vice versa) and introduce a sense of playfulness via strange, archaic objects that stimulate the imagination.

WOOD, CLAY AND CONCRETE
A rustic French stoneware jug of flowers has a wealth of rich tones within its mottled glaze; the wooden children's shoe lasts add a sweet touch, each one telling its own story (opposite).

STEPPED SILHOUETTE
Our new design for reworked apple crates as shelving is arranged in a stepped formation, with an industrial cage light hanging over the void. The pendant light's strong silhouette finds a pairing with the floor lamp, made in our workshop from a music stand combined with a brioche tin shade.

WORK ON CANVAS
In our workroom/studio, thick canvas panels, hanging from the beams, divide up the space (this page). The canvas organizer pockets attached provide extra storage space.

NATURALLY DERIVED
We always seek out unusually shaped wooden objects, regardless of their original use. Opposite, clockwise from top left: a hat block sits next to an empty frame and a couple of wooden cogs, one forming the base of a domed light fitting; earthenware shows the hand of its maker in its slightly uneven lines; papery plaited/braided garlic in an unusual purple hue; ceramics look just as attractive filling a bowl as they do lined up neatly on a shelf.

A LESS-IS-MORE ATTITUDE OFFERS A CHANCE TO CONTEMPLATE THE INNATE QUALITIES OF NATURAL MATERIALS, AND THE CRAFTSMANSHIP BEHIND HANDMADE OBJECTS.

AUTUMNAL COLOURS
A branch of autumnal beech, in shades of copper and olive green, tones in with the mellow russet of a pair of turned sycamore bowls. One bowl has been upended to display its deep grain, which is remarkably similar to the dark veins on each leaf.

BLUSH & GLOW

Pip Rau has been collecting and dealing in Central Asian and Afghan textiles since the 1970s. Her clients are private collectors, interior designers and costume designers for film and television, and her esteemed collection of Central Asian ikats merited its own show at London's Victoria and Albert Museum. For as long as she has been dealing in textiles, Pip has lived in a handsome, stuccoed house in North London – initially in the building's first-floor apartment, but she gradually bought the other apartments and expanded into them. Having given up her Islington shop, Pip's house is now home and showroom in one, and mixes the rich, dark tones so beloved of the Victorians with the vibrant hues of her splendid textiles.

{feature home}

RICH AND EXOTIC
Pip Rau's textile collection is richly coloured, sourced from lands where fabrics provide a cheering shot of brightness. Their richness is accentuated by layering them together, like the rail of Afghan robes (above), or creating an equally colourful backdrop for them, as in the master bedroom (opposite), where glowing Indian red walls match 19th-century suzanis from Tashkent.

These two worlds sit remarkably well together; Pip's bedroom, a deep Indian red, would surely have pleased the Victorians, and yet it also goes beautifully with the 19th-century suzanis from Tashkent, which hang above and behind the bed, with another forming a bedspread. The curtains, wall hangings and other trinkets feature pink, scarlet, crimson and every other shade of red, so the whole room becomes an exercise in layering up a single colour – a feast for the eyes.

Pip's showroom and stockroom feature stacks of textiles: kilims in shades of russet, dark brown and blue, and rack upon rack of Afghan robes. One shelf is dedicated to the corduroy shirts traditionally worn by Turkmen, patched up here and there with contrasting colourful embroidery. The ikat robes are eye-wateringly bright, featuring up to seven colours, and often with a contrasting pattern on the lining, yet they don't jar. This has a lot to do with the dyeing and weaving techniques – one colour blurs fuzzily into another – as well as each pattern having unique irregularities.

Textiles are treated as works of art here, and their craftsmanship and asymmetry are what makes them just as interesting to look at as a painting or drawing. Textiles create warmth in a house, and here their hand-craftedness also provides a foil for the high ceilings and intricate plaster mouldings. These are valuable antiques placed in a rather grand setting, but the visitor does not for a minute feel intimidated by it all. This has much to do with the fact that the house is infused with Pip's spirited personality, but it's also about the humanity that emanates from all the handmade objects within.

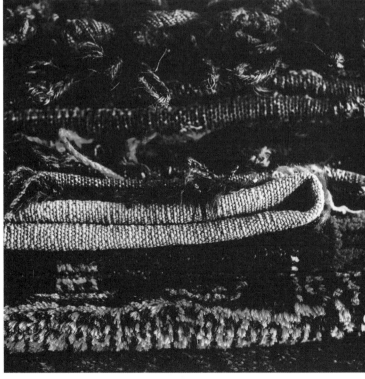

POLISHED PERFORMANCE
The reception room (opposite) has opulent polished plaster walls left their natural shade – a creamy nude – and are adorned with rare ikat textiles. The mismatched quality of the hand-dyed seat pads on the bergère sofa and chairs adds a sense of bohemian informality.

COLOUR COMPOSURE
Despite the riot of colour at play (above right), the objects possess a natural harmony.

THREADS OF TRADITION
A pile of carpets shows a more subdued side (right): muddy browns and dark blues, enlivened by a lick of orange.

121

LOW LIFE

Pip's living room dispenses with sofas in favour of lounging on an Afghan sleeping rug (this page); the cushions were originally saddlebags, used by nomadic people for carrying their possessions. The fine detail and rich colours of the Turkish kilim on the wall make it one of the finest textiles in the house.

PATTERN MAKING

Central Asia's love of pattern sings out from every object. Opposite, clockwise from top left: fruitwood bowls on a Turkmen chest with a 1950s lamp; the master bedroom, a riot of pinks and reds; stacked ikat robes; wooden cooking implements in a 200-year-old bowl blackened with age.

OPULENT BATHING
Designed and decorated by Pip's collaborator Clive Richardson, the downstairs cloakroom has an original Victorian basin and taps/faucets. The towel warmer, hanging on the ultramarine polished plaster walls, is made from old copper plumbing pipes – a touch that the inventive Victorians would probably have appreciated.

Q&A

Perfect or imperfect? Imperfect.

Is there anything in your home you would consider 'perfectly imperfect'? Everything in my house is imperfect, and I love it that way. I am drawn to pieces that come with a story – that have a sense of history and a previous life.

Do you have a favourite object in your house? What is it, and where did it come from? I have an early 19th-century ikat that I bought in Kabul in the 1970s. This is an example of basic design that has worn well over the years, and although it is slightly threadbare in places, I appreciate it all the more for that. It hangs in my living room.

How would you spend the ideal day at home? I enjoy spending time surrounded by the objects I have collected over the years, and I have many happy memories of travelling. It is an ideal environment in which to relax. I love having friends here and we've had some great parties.

Likes: Travelling. Shopping in markets. Art galleries and exhibitions.

Dislikes: Racism. Pretentiousness. Organized religion. Cats. Geraniums.

What music do you enjoy listening to? Fleetwood Mac, Bach and all sorts.

What's the biggest talking point in your home when people visit? I suppose the rooms that spark the most interest are the Minton-tiled bathroom and the large drawing room with polished marble walls, French doors at the bay window and a curved wooden door.

There is joy in the act of making — regardless of the artistic merit of the end result — but there is also a lifetime of pleasure to be had from enjoying the fruits of others' labour. It is easy to admire the high level of skill, perhaps passed down through generations, that goes into embroidering a suzani wall hanging or making a porcelain pot so thin that it seems magically infused with daylight. The *wabi-sabi* home also champions more workaday handmade objects. Although we live in a mass-produced world, it is relatively easy and inexpensive to introduce, say, a few carved spoons for the kitchen, or woven bowls for storing small treasures. You may also gain more pleasure from seemingly prosaic things, because you touch and use them every day.

Craft is an important component of *wabi-sabi*. Anything that bears the hand of its maker, from stitching to brush strokes, instills a sense of authenticity and honesty; it literally bestows on your home the human touch. As many of our lives become more and more removed from the physical world and face-to-face relationships, craft is a vital touchstone. Handmade and mass-produced can also make a winning combination — place a mid-century light beside a hand-turned bowl and one will throw the other into relief, the contrast bringing out the best in both.

{handmade}

CRAFTED

The handmade can often be thrifty and ingenious in its reuse of things that are leftover or forgotten. Many of the people featured in this book have used their creative skills to add a handmade element, from using scraps of old fabric to wrap around wire coat-hangers to skilled cabinetmaking. It is their way of creating a home that is tailor-made to their needs and tastes. And although making or reinventing your own possessions is not a requirement for the *wabi-sabi* home, it will give you a degree of enrichment that is hard to match.

{smooth & chiselled wood}

TURNED

Warm, tactile and full of character, wood's irregularities of grain and colour make it one of the most distinctive features of a *wabi-sabi* interior. It ages wonderfully, looking good even when blackened or cracked with age. Handmade wooden objects have a special quality that connects us to their maker and gives them an innate humanity. Seek out wooden versions of everyday items – bowls, spoons and other utensils – and you will be rewarded every time you use them. Turned and carved wood have rather different qualities. Made using a lathe, turned objects have more regularity and intricacy about them, as well as a smoothness that can be burnished to an alluring glow with the addition of oil or wax. Carved items, meanwhile, have a rustic energy that springs directly from the tools, and the hands, that made them.

HANDMADE WOODEN OBJECTS HAVE A SPECIAL QUALITY THAT CONNECTS US TO THEIR MAKER AND GIVES THEM AN INNATE HUMANITY.

WORN AND WEATHERED

In all these simply made and unadorned wooden objects (this page and opposite), you can clearly see the hand of their maker – it is this irregularity that makes them so beautiful. Their rawness and unpolished nature mean that with daily use they will soon take on a new patina.

ROUGH WITH THE SMOOTH

The plain weathered planks and roughly cast wall are the perfect foil for the artisan makers at the Japanese store Outbound. The shelves, supported on metal pegs, are a simple idea that works very well (right). Smooth wooden spoons by Ryuji Mitani (opposite below left) contrast well with the silvered planks. The oversized Yale key (above right) and forks (opposite above right) are from our collection of Folk Art.

HAND TOOLS CAN BE ADMIRED FOR BEING WELL CRAFTED, BUT THEY ALSO INVITE IDEAS ABOUT WHO USED THEM AND WHAT THEY MADE.

GENTLE CURVES

Japanese craftsman Jiro Suda has an obvious love of, and affinity with, wood. His elm bowls, seen here on display at Japanese store Outbound, have elegant undulating rims that echo the gently curving grain of the wood (previous spread). It is lovely to trace over them with a finger. Each bowl is different because each tree is different – the raw material suggests the form.

HAND-HELD

We have always been fascinated with tools; this oversized trowel (this page) once adorned an old ironmongers. Tools can be admired for being well crafted, but they also invite ideas about who used them and what they made.

HANDMADE

The dance of the axe around a piece of wood begins the process of spoon-making before whittling begins. Ryuji Mitani's smooth wooden spoons (opposite) are the culmination of years of perfecting his craft.

ONE OF THE JOYS OF RUSTIC WOODEN FURNITURE IS THAT YOU CAN OFTEN SEE EXACTLY HOW IT HAS BEEN MADE.

INSTANT UNDERSTANDING

One of the joys of rustic wooden furniture is that you can often see exactly how it has been made, perhaps held together with chunky dowels or, more elegantly, with a dovetail joint. There's something inherently soothing about gleaning that instant level of understanding. In Masato Hori's Tokyo store Sam L Waltz, the shelving, fruit crates, tables and benches (opposite) share these easy-to-read characteristics, as does the table at Outbound (right). The two chairs (above left and right) seem to be having a long-distance conversation, one on a Tokyo balcony, the other in our home in Herefordshire.

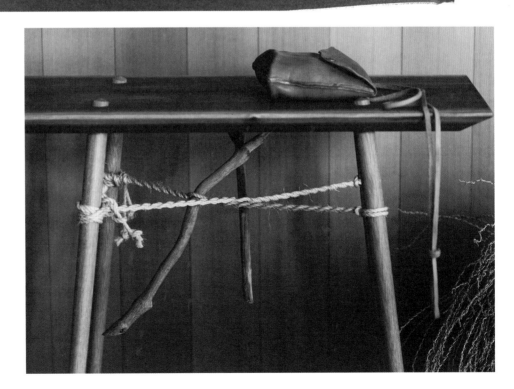

CERAMICS MADE ON A WHEEL SEEM TO HAVE INVESTED IN THEM SOME OF THE WHIRRING ENERGY THAT WENT INTO THEIR MAKING.

{crazed, uneven ceramics}

THROWN

Thrown ceramics – that is, made on a wheel – seem to have invested in them some of the whirring energy that went into their making. Symmetrical perfection is possible using this method, but rarely desirable: the soft dents and gentle lines in the clay are the threads that tie it to its maker. The philosophy of *wabi-sabi* – finding beauty in imperfection – is never better illustrated than in Japanese ceramics. For centuries, uneven, asymmetrical vessels have been seen as the correct accompaniment to the refined ritual of the tea ceremony; *hagi* pottery is particularly prized for the way the tea stains the crazed glazing, changing it over time. Glazing on any ceramics, from French stoneware to English slipware, adds an additional layer of uncertainty during firing, with each object emerging as a perfectly unique marriage of chemistry and craft.

MASTERS IN CLAY

Architect Wataru Ohashi's hard-wearing ceramics for everyday use are spread out on the wooden shelves in his office (above). Some of the exceptional Japanese ceramicists under the wing of Hitomi Yoshimura at Zakka include Keisuke Iwata, who made most of the items on these shelves (right). The bowls (middle shelf, left) are by Junsuke Asai; the teacup and saucer (top shelf, centre) by Tokashi Yamanobe.

URBAN-RUSTIC KITCHEN

Zakka's kitchen area (opposite) contains a monumental baker's table and wooden cupboards that would seem more at home below stairs in a stately home than an urban Japanese store. The stainless-steel worktop and extractor, and spun-metal pendant lights offer a contrasting industrial aesthetic.

NORIKO INOMOTO'S APARTMENT IS TYPICAL FOR TOKYO IN ITS COMPACTNESS, BUT SHE KEEPS EVERYTHING ON DISPLAY RATHER THAN SHUTTING IT AWAY.

SMALL PLEASURES

Florist and stylist Noriko Inomoto's apartment (this page) is typical for Tokyo in its compactness, but she keeps everything on display rather than shutting it away. The shelf of the stainless-steel kitchen work station is bursting with bamboo steamers and cooking pots, while the countertop is reserved for European-style glazed white ceramics. Sometimes a single statement vessel is all that's needed, like this waisted vase (opposite) in the Japanese store Ensyu. Set against roughly papered and whitewashed walls, its stark monochrome is picked up by the black-and-white table.

CERAMICS AS ART

We collect Dylan Bowen's highly distinctive slipware pieces (this page and opposite), which are joyously expressive in their glazed daubings. The 'slip', a mix of clay and water, is painted on the piece, with a glaze applied over the top, to give the yellow and brown colouring. This very old technique has found new life in Dylan's hands, with echoes of both the folky slipware of the 17th century and contemporary abstract art. This blending of old and new traditions is possibly the reason that his work fits into our home so well.

PART OF THE ART

Propping up paintings rather than hanging them means that any objects placed in front almost become part of the artwork, like the narcissus stems framed by the black vase in Cornish painter David Pearce's work (left). His paintings have the same sort of spontaneous vigour as Dylan Bowen's glossy slipware flasks displayed in front. The dark brown jug is by studio potter Andrew Crouch. The earthenware bowl in Noriko Inomoto's home (above), with its elegant footed shape, is a *chawan* (tea bowl), used in tea ceremonies and prized for its subtle imperfections.

147

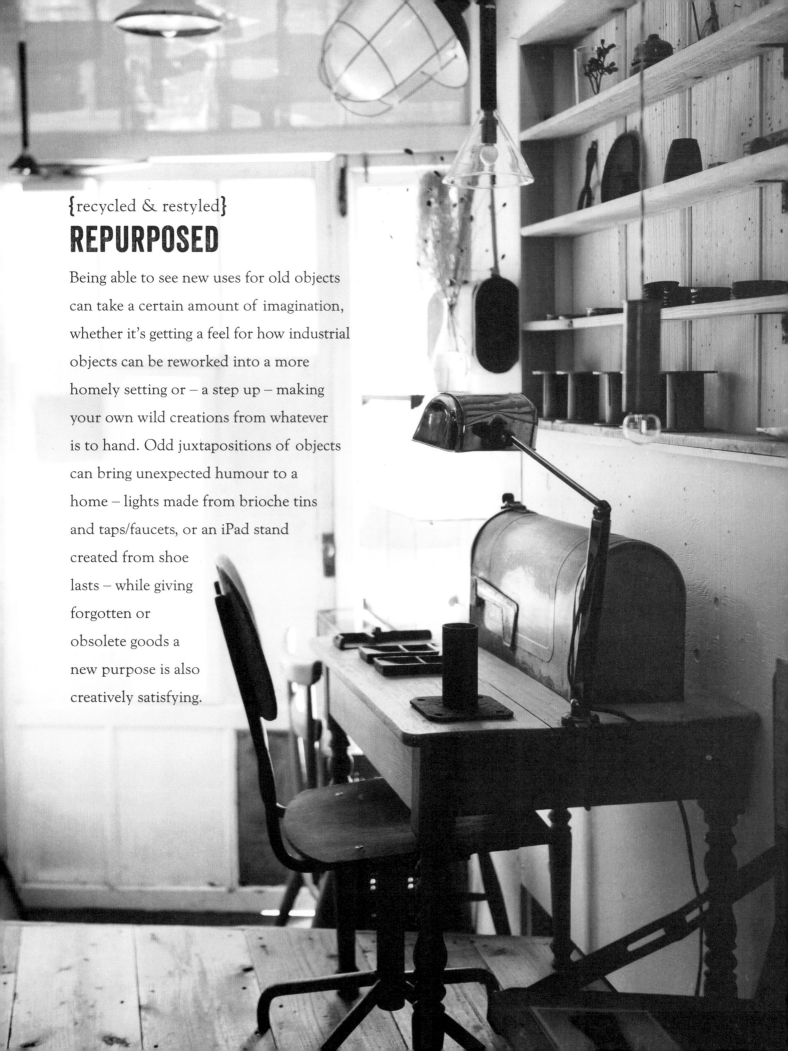

{recycled & restyled}

REPURPOSED

Being able to see new uses for old objects can take a certain amount of imagination, whether it's getting a feel for how industrial objects can be reworked into a more homely setting or – a step up – making your own wild creations from whatever is to hand. Odd juxtapositions of objects can bring unexpected humour to a home – lights made from brioche tins and taps/faucets, or an iPad stand created from shoe lasts – while giving forgotten or obsolete goods a new purpose is also creatively satisfying.

NEW WAYS TO PLAY

Die-cast toys sitting at the bottom of backless wooden frames play with scale (this page). The offset, stacked arrangement results in a carefree look, which is supported by the playfulness of the toys themselves. An American mailbox with a saddle of rust (opposite) has been repurposed as an office storage box in Masakazu Yonehara's store Buaisou. The desk, chair and lighting are all redundant factory finds.

TOP TABLE

Trestle legs are one of the easiest ways to turn a flat object into a working table. Scaffold boards or an old door can simply be laid on top, and if you find something else you would rather use, it's easy to change. The trestle table in Masato Hori's Tokyo store Sam L Waltz (this page) has old fruit crates stored underneath, while ours (opposite) is topped with ware boards and Mark's homemade and irreverent iPad holder.

EVOLUTIONARY CHAIR

At the heart of this piece of furniture is a pine flat-pack chair, called Third, by British designer Max Lamb. Kazuto Kobayashi (of Tokyo's Outbound store) assembled it but went further, building an arm and an extended base from old crates and wood, and finally strapping on some hessian as a seat pad. The result has the look of something that has evolved, as if the pale, new wood has grown out of the gnarled old wood.

REINVENTION NEEDN'T INVOLVE DIY SKILLS; ALL THAT'S
REQUIRED IS THE ABILITY TO SEE THE POTENTIAL IN SOMETHING.

RETHINKING THE ORDINARY

Reinvention needn't involve DIY
skills; all that's required is the
ability to see the potential in
something. Clockwise from above
left: a low-fi calendar, made by
Hiroki Kitade from stones, shells
and sand in a wooden tray,
looks like a Japanese garden in
miniature; a piece of weathered
wood on a metal stand makes
for an informal shop sign outside
Tokyo store Buaisou; a deeply
grooved piece of driftwood makes
a practical soap dish in Costanza
Algranti's Milan home; Mark's
lighting, made from sliced-off wine
bottles, suspended with old-
fashioned, fabric-covered cable.

153

ARTISAN MAKER

Ryuji Mitani is a well-known craftsman – he makes wooden tableware such as trays, spoons, forks and bowls – but he is also passionate about promoting Japanese crafts, curating exhibitions and writing books. His home, gallery and studio in the picturesque Japanese city of Matsumoto are testimony to the simple pleasure that can be gleaned from being surrounded by handmade things. Ryuji's home is not overfilled with objects, which means that you really notice the detail of what is on show: the careful chisel marks inside a bowl, the patina of a leather chair, the folds in a snowy white cotton curtain.

PERFECT SIMPLICITY
Ryuji Mitani's home-cum-studio is like a still life: items are put together in a studied way, with nothing superfluous or out of place. Simplicity is the main theme. There is no pattern or decoration, so the eyes notice shape and texture – like the leather-tied flask and hand-thrown teapots that sit on one of Ruyji's hand-carved wooden trays (above left).

CRAFTED KITCHEN

The mellow, tawny wood tones of mid-century furniture contrast with Ryuji's paler kitchen cabinetry (opposite and this page). He made the kitchen units himself, and they are as minimally effective as the bowls and other smaller items for which he is so admired.

PLAY TO THE GALLERY

In a house with little or no art on the walls, the open shelving, full of books and stacked-up kitchenware, provides the decorative interest (this page). A simple palette of white paint and wood turns every object into a work of art, and when these are handmade, you want to look closer.

QUIET AND HONEST

There's an honesty to this home that is echoed in the objects within it. Exposed beams and a chunky flue on the stove (opposite left) and a white enamelled light (opposite right) speak of the owner's love of the unadorned. The only bright colour comes from the fresh greenery in the garden, leading the eye outside.

RYUJI MAY WORK WITH SOME AGE-OLD TECHNIQUES, BUT THE
HOUSE AS A WHOLE HAS A CONTEMPORARY MINIMALISM ABOUT IT.

Nearly everything on display here is functional, and Ryuji's studio, workshop and living space all blend seamlessly. His craftsman's tools are elevated to the status of artworks. They are mounted on the wall in neat rows, their silhouettes either picked out against a white background or lined up along the floor. The traditional tools and old woodworking machines are conspicuously worn examples and good storytellers. They seem to invite questions about how they were used, the hands that held them and the objects they once made.

In its simplicity, Japanese craftsmanship often has the ability to create an ageless feel in a home; Ryuji may work with some age-old techniques, but the house as a whole has a contemporary minimalism about it, mixing industrial enamel lighting and examples of mid-century furniture. He has also used his skill with wood to make

some of the cabinetry to his own specification, including the beautifully spare and understated kitchen units. Naturally, wood plays a large part throughout the interior, both in the fabric of the building – the timber floorboards and window frames – and the objects inside it, from the scuffed desk to the open shelving.

Nothing is superfluous here – a chair has its place because it will be sat on, not so it will fill up a corner or add a decorative flourish. Bowls, kitchenware and teapots are all there to be used, which very much ties in with Ryuji's wider philosophy: he says that his turned and chiselled bowls are meant for regular use, not special occasions. He understands that those items we cook with and eat with every day should, ideally, be handmade – not simply for the reason they offer tactile pleasure, but because they connect us together as people.

PLAY OF NEUTRALS
This corner of the house focuses on a play of neutral shades: the dull steel of the wood-burning stove, the timber floor and the off-white curtain. It has a quiet, monastic feel, serving just the basic needs of sleeping and keeping warm.

NEARLY EVERYTHING ON DISPLAY IS FUNCTIONAL, APART FROM RYUJI'S DELICATE WATERCOLOURS, WHICH ARE CASUALLY PINNED TO THE WALL.

BANISH STRAIGHT LINES

Ryuji's lacquer studio has an abundance of natural light. This is where he mixes his pigments with gum-like white sap from the urushi tree before applying it in layers to his work (above). The upturned bowls are left to dry on shelves after each layer of urushi lacquer has been applied (right). It takes up to 24 hours between each coat, which results in a deep, rich, glossy finish. Open shelves display his abstract bowls and plates in monochrome tones, except for the large blood red tray (above right).

TOOLS OF THE TRADE

True to the *wabi-sabi* philosophy, Ryuji's workshop is presented with the same care and precision as the living spaces, with tools silhouetted against the walls (this page and opposite). Their curious shapes invite closer inspection, while their age-worn markings tell the hidden story of the many objects they have made. Here, everything seems to have its place – the product of a single, highly organized mind – and it is refreshing to know that, far from being the outdated tools of long-forgotten production processes, these objects are still used, and loved, every day.

Q&A

Do you have your own philosophy of life?
I like everyday simplicity and comfort. I can't change the whole world, but I hope that my wooden pieces will bring simplicity and comfort to someone's life.

What music do you enjoy listening to?
Piano music by Keith Jarrett and Bill Evans.

Which authors or books inspire you? *Saigo no Shinran* ('The Last Shinran') by Takaaki Yoshimoto, *Mon* ('The Gate') by Soseki Natsume and *Onnatachiyo* ('Ladies') by Jyuzo Itami.

What are you reading at the moment? *How To Count the Friend Poem* by Hiroshi Osada and *No One Belongs Here More Than You* by Miranda July.

Likes: Carrying the table outside and having lunch in the shade of a tree. Meals with friends. Textiles and baskets woven with care. White porcelain and linen sheets. Well-used wooden vessels and chairs.

Do you have any recipes that you like?
Yes – pasta with *negi* (Japanese leeks). You will need olive oil, crushed garlic, thinly sliced leeks and some pasta. Pour a generous amount of olive oil into a pan and add the garlic. Cook over a low heat until soft, then add the thinly sliced leeks and continue to cook gently until they are soft. Bring a pan of water to the boil and add a pinch of salt. Add the pasta to the boiling water. Once the pasta is ready, drain then add it to the leek mixture, combine and serve.

Displaying objects in your home is a way to express your personal passions, as you turn generic spaces into places infused with your own unique style. For many, the process of arranging (and rearranging) items is nothing short of therapy, and is as much a part of the fun as stepping back and admiring the appealingly balanced results.

Collections allow you to play at being your very own curator, picking and choosing what looks best together, but unlike in a museum or gallery, no one is judging your belongings on artistic merit alone. *Wabi-sabi* holds that no object is too modest for display. Sometimes it's just about looking beyond the obvious function of something – from a watering can to a pair of shoes – and seeing instead its silhouette, colour or patina, and, crucially, how it looks next to other objects.

Displaying everyday items out of context can make you see them in a completely different way. Objects that seem unremarkable on their own, such as a coloured glass tumbler, can turn into a feast for the eyes when stacked up in large numbers. Balancing a group of seemingly disparate things is an art, but the trick is usually to make sure they are not too different. Experiment with shape, scale, texture and materials to achieve a visually stimulating but harmonious grouping.

{collections}

GATHERED

If you live in a small space, where every inch counts, make your collections less decorative and more functional. Old trunks grouped together, for example, create valuable storage and visual impact, while bowls and bread boards can still be highly practical. Or embrace the art of micro-collecting; Masakazu and Masayo placed tiny letterpress blocks in the cracks in their floorboards (see page 65). Like the best collections, this creates an intriguing narrative that fires the imagination and makes you lean in for a closer look.

{random found objects}

FOUND

Quite a large proportion of the objects in our own home were never made for a domestic setting. Some originally had a commercial or industrial purpose – shop signs and shoe lasts, fishing floats and school chairs – while others are 'found' in the truest sense, such as feathers, stones and hazel sticks. It is precisely their 'otherness' that creates the excitement and tells a story. We believe that anything with a sense of narrative has a place in your home, regardless of its origin: things that have aged in an interesting way, or make you ask questions about what they could have been in a previous life or how they might have once been used, all add another line to the story. Building up a quantity of a single type of found object often unlocks their decorative potential, so keep collecting whatever catches your eye until you've reached a critical mass.

WE BELIEVE THAT ANYTHING WITH A SENSE OF NARRATIVE HAS A PLACE IN YOUR HOME, REGARDLESS OF ITS ORIGIN.

CURIOUS OBJECTS
Introducing found objects creates a sense of the unexpected, especially when they are juxtaposed with more conventional items. A birdcage is a lovely object, even without a feathered inmate (opposite left). Obsolete printers' trays are common finds these days and make excellent display cases for smaller items; this one in Anna Phillips' home has been selectively lined with endpapers (opposite right). Brass and steel scissors are deemed worthy objects to display next to more domestic ones at Masato Hori's store in Tokyo (this page).

SHOES ARE SOME OF THE MOST EVOCATIVE OBJECTS OF ALL, RETAINING THE SHAPE AND 'ESSENCE' OF THE WEARER.

COLLECTIONS IN THE MAKING

The studio at the top of our farmhouse is where collections take shape, acting as a temporary home to groups of objects from pearl-handled knives to 1950s globes (opposite). Shoes are some of the most evocative objects of all, because they retain the shape and 'essence' of the wearer. A group of canvas tap shoes hot-foot it along a radiator (above). Mark gets very excited when he finds shoes stuffed with old tissue or newspaper (right) – a sign of how carefully they were looked after by their former owner.

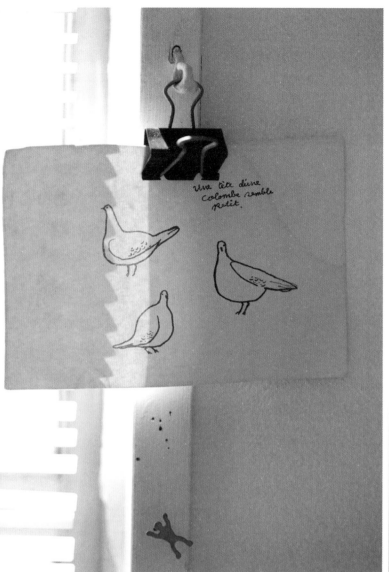

DISPLAY FOR TODAY

Wataru Ohashi has three pigeons that visit his balcony every day. This *kawaii* (Japanese for 'cute') drawing, hanging from a bulldog clip, is his interpretation of them (above left). The arrangement on Pip Rau's mantelpiece has remained unchanged for years, and is a truly multicultural gathering, including a Coptic cross from Istanbul, a little Russian icon and figures from India. Just seen on the wall is an early 19th-century suzani, rare for its age and an unusual square shape (above).

THE ARRANGEMENT ON PIP RAU'S MANTELPIECE IS A TRULY MULTICULTURAL GATHERING, INCLUDING A COPTIC CROSS FROM ISTANBUL, A LITTLE RUSSIAN ICON AND FIGURES FROM INDIA.

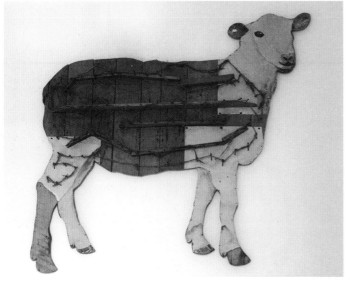

SEE THE SIGN

Signage and other ephemera originally used in retail make for eye-catching additions – after all, attracting attention was their first purpose – and they are often well made, designed for a life in the elements. The distinctive red, blue and white stripes of a barber's pole (above) add some interest and colour to our weathered table. The large cog has been made into a mirror frame. Placing the industrial lamp across it amplifies the light when it's turned on.

IN LIKE A LAMB

Antiques textile dealer Katharine Pole couldn't resist buying this placid sheep (left) – a nail-studded wooden board strung with wool, with a painted face – in the south of France. She doesn't know what it was used for, but half the fun is guessing: a shop sign, perhaps? Iconography from a church?

171

GUIDE THE EYE

More collections taking shape in our studio (left
and above). The white walls and seagrass matting
are a good blank canvas for the ever-changing scene,
with every surface of the table covered with desirable
objects. They all belong on the same colour spectrum,
with russet, woody tones highlighted by the strings
of shell necklaces, originally from Africa. The rustic
ceramics are from Hungary, which has a strong
tradition of folk pottery. Giving the whole arrangement
a vertical thrust are the carved wood architraves and
Mark's quirky tripod lamps, which fill up the whole
space and guide the eye around.

{useful everyday objects}

EVERYDAY

Wabi-sabi finds beauty and peace in simple everyday items and many of the homes featured in this book use open shelving to display practical tools and utensils alongside more decorative items – all are treated equally. If you aim for less plastic and more natural materials, such as wood, bamboo, reed and cork, the open shelving will automatically create a greater sense of harmony. Do away with the idea that you should save 'best' china or glassware for special occasions, and try to use your nicest things all the time. Ideally, they should be tactile and handmade: daily contact with hand-thrown bowls or bone-handled cutlery/flatware, for example, will give a little satisfaction, spread over a long, long time.

SHELF LIFE

Compulsive collector Masato Hori travels through
Europe and Scandinavia to source stock for his
two Tokyo stores, Cinq and Sam L Waltz, but many
of his finds end up in his studio, where he also
occasionally sleeps. The night before our visit to
photograph his store and studio, Masato had been
up until 4am rearranging his shelves (opposite and
this page). He greeted us bleary eyed but happy.
He is the ultimate committed collector.

THE JEWEL-LIKE GLASS CASTS TINTED SHADOWS ON THE WALL. STACKING ONE OR MORE PIECES CREATES LAYERS OF DIFFERENT COLOURS.

COLOUR CAST
Masato's collections of stoneware and Swedish glassware (opposite). The jewel-like glass casts tinted shadows on the wall. Sacking one or more pieces creates layers of different colours.

MINIATURE WORLDS
In Anna Phillips' home, jars of paint pigment sit on top of a box-shaped shelf that has been transformed into a little room by the addition of a toy table and chair (above). Its emerald green colour is picked up in the middle jar. Architect Wataru Ohashi's intricate paper models of his buildings, lined up on the shelves of his office, make an intriguing display (above right). Matchbox labels are like windows onto social history, reflecting the graphic trends of the time within a few square inches. Some of Masato's collection is stored in a wooden toy truck (right).

FIELD OF PLAY

Masato collects and sells guitars, which he buys in Europe. In his store, they are treated like the works of art that they are, mounted on the wall in a pleasing threesome (this page).The fact that they are not quite identical makes it a much more satisfying display, as the eye is kept busy picking out their differences in size, finish and detailing.

GAINFUL EMPLOYMENT

Wataru's meticulously organized office (opposite) is dominated by a modular storage system of stacked boxes, full of buff-coloured boxes and files, magazines and books.

PUT TO GOOD USE

These brushes (right) were mostly bought in Tokyu
Hands, a chain of Japanese department stores that
sells crafts, stationery and homewares, with an
emphasis on basic, practical products, such as the
bamboo-handled brushes and sisal string. Laid together
on the table, they seem to offer the promise of creative
fulfilment, ready to spring into action and serve their
given purpose at any moment. This is a small part of
our collection of wooden rulers, some of them folding
with tarnished brass hinges (above). They are still sold
new – and have barely changed – but the old ones are
imbued with a sense of time and a life of industry.

{nature/temporary displays}

EPHEMERAL

Wabi-sabi celebrates the transient beauty of the natural world. There is imperfection inherent in always-growing, always-decaying nature, and an awareness of this constant flux is a good thing to introduce at home, because it connects us with the world outside. Instead of pristine bunches of flowers, discarded as soon as they droop, embrace plants that are just as interesting as they die, like the lacy casing of a Chinese lantern or an architecturally arresting spiked teasel. Experiment with single blooms in unusual vessels, so that one does not overpower the other, or emphasize nature's uncontrollable side with trailing branches that seem to take over.

CALL OF THE WILD

A papery dried flower stem on a stainless-steel worktop (previous spread, left). Dry your own flowers by hanging them upside down, somewhere warm and out of sunlight, for a few weeks. Ivy springs from a glass bottle and winds its way over a stone table (previous spread, right). This plant looks especially beautiful in autumn, when it sports starbursts of light green flowers.

ARTLESS ARRANGEMENT

Flowers are an easy way to introduce bright, temporary colour to your home. Seasonal blooms with interesting silhouettes – iris and honeysuckle – are placed sparingly in an assortment of glasses and jars along a white mantelpiece. The arrangement looks very informal, but some thought has gone into the rising and falling shape of the overall grouping (above). There is a freshness to this unusual combination of old chemists' bottles filled with stems of greenery, perched on an old, worn machinist's chair in the shop window at Tokyo store Ensyu (opposite). Gathered directly from outside, the stems make a simple, clear connection between the inside space and the wider world in a way that air-freighted, out-of-season flowers cannot.

IN BALANCE
Stylist and florist Noriko
Inomoto has a talent for
balancing plants and flowers
with their vessels, often in a
minimalist way. The tall vase
contains a fruiting olive branch
and a pansy peeking out of the
top; at its base, a pansy rests in
a tiny pot. The terracotta bottle
echoes the Mediterranean
origins of the olives.

SIMPLE STEMS

Green stems in a preserving jar make the simplest arrangement at Japanese store Zakka (above left); test-tube and wire stem vases are useful for showcasing single stems, like ivy (above); upturned terracotta pots on a Tokyo balcony are an out-of-season still life (left).

NATURE IN THE CITY

Outside Tokyo store Okura, famous for its indigo-dyed clothing and textiles, a squat glass vase in a wire-framed planter, once an oil lamp, is filled with rice grass. Large, denim-wrapped pots, also containing grass, add a sense of abundant nature, in contrast to the sober corrugated-tin façade (following spread).

OUTDOOR CRAFTS

The Japanese village of Mashiko is home to Starnet, a gallery and studio that shows local work. An outdoor cooking area contains an inviting circle of tree-trunk seats and a stone outdoor sink (pages 190–1).

HUNTER-GATHERER

Two hours north of Tokyo is the weekend home of antiques dealer and interior designer Shotaro Yoshida and his stylist partner Midori Takahashi. This renovated taxi station, built in the 1930s, is also a shopfront for their business, Tamiser, where visitors can browse and buy. It's an unusual concept for Japan, where domestic privacy is guarded and space is restricted, but away from the city there is more freedom to spread out – and more freedom to collect and display. Books, kitchenware, glass and other objects are given the same visual weight as curious abstract pieces, all set against an airy industrial backdrop.

{feature home}

NEATLY ORGANIZED

A busy but supremely efficient kitchen is as much a place for display as it is for cooking. The trolley (above and opposite), an industrial substitute for a traditional kitchen island, heaves with cutlery/flatware and dishes. Smooth, 'colder' materials, like the stainless-steel sink and concrete floor, contrast with worn, patinated, obviously handmade objects.

SHOTARO ADMITS TO BEING A PERFECTIONIST, WHILE APPRECIATING
THE NEED FOR HIS HOME TO BE A LITTLE LOOSE AROUND THE EDGES.

Industrial conversions often have simple, honest construction methods and an amazing quantity of natural light. Shotaro and Midori's home is the same, with the light flooding in across the mostly open-plan interior. Exposed rafters and timber-clad walls, all whitewashed, offer regularity and rhythm in a space that is irregular in so many other ways, such as the jigsaw puzzle of different-sized doors and windows that acts as a divider between the living space and store. Shotaro enhances this look with such things as the huge factory trolley in the kitchen that acts as a monumental island. The metal bunk beds are original to the building, and were once used by off-duty taxi drivers.

UP IN THE RAFTERS
The kitchen storage (opposite) is built almost into the rafters, with open shelving giving a sense of uniformity, despite the various shapes and sizes of the crockery and glassware on display.

EARTHY HARMONY
Using a limited palette of materials is one way to achieve harmony when gathering lots of objects together. Ceramics, glass and wood come together (above left and right) to create a rustic-looking combination. Everything is clearly well used, but no less attractive for it.

Shotaro's background in antiques makes him a past master at creating a sense of coherence out of a collection of one-off objects. Mid-century design books are shown with their covers outwards. Industrial objects are placed against the whitewashed walls to enhance their silhouettes. Most things are simple, functional and handmade, which ties everything together, albeit in a subliminal way. The lack of soft furnishings could make the place feel stark, but the use of natural materials warm it up a little. This is Shotaro and Midori's take on a simple, rustic retreat – it is not minimal, yet it is arranged in such a self-assured way that it emanates order and calm.

HUMBLE ROOTS
Whitewashed woodwork
provides a uniform backdrop
for an eclectic mix of
furniture (this page and
opposite). Humble pieces,
such as the long table of
reclaimed wood surrounded
by mid-century Finnish stools,
is a good fit for the building,
which has unpretentious roots
as a taxi-drivers' station.

FLEXIBLE LIVING
Bulky pieces of furniture on castors are a great way to break up large, open-plan rooms and also allow you to quickly reconfigure them. This half-whitewashed shelving is just the right height – the light from the upper windows can still come in over the top of it – and it screens the metal bunk beds, where the taxi drivers used to sleep, from the rest of the space.

AS THEIR HOME HAS NO INTERIOR WALLS, SHOTARO AND MIDORI HAVE USED IMAGINATIVE WAYS TO CREATE A FLEXIBLE SPACE IN WHICH TO LIVE AND WORK.

DISPLAYING ONE-OFFS

Shotaro and Midori are masters at finding inventive ways to display one-off, seemingly disparate objects. Smaller treasures are reserved for a display case (above left), while some books are shown, library-style, with their fronts facing outwards – their pictorial covers act as artwork and are easily interchangeable (above right). The rough, scuffed walls in the bathroom (far left) and the trough-like basin (left) keep with the overall theme of industrial-influenced imperfection.

199

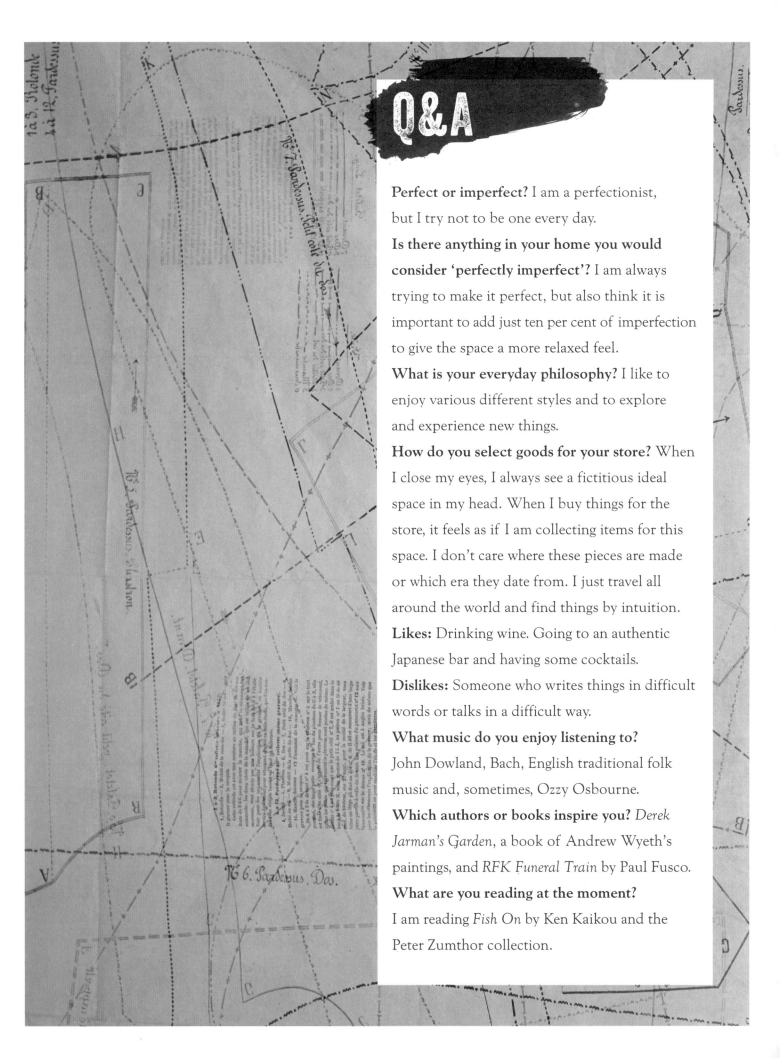

Q&A

Perfect or imperfect? I am a perfectionist, but I try not to be one every day.

Is there anything in your home you would consider 'perfectly imperfect'? I am always trying to make it perfect, but also think it is important to add just ten per cent of imperfection to give the space a more relaxed feel.

What is your everyday philosophy? I like to enjoy various different styles and to explore and experience new things.

How do you select goods for your store? When I close my eyes, I always see a fictitious ideal space in my head. When I buy things for the store, it feels as if I am collecting items for this space. I don't care where these pieces are made or which era they date from. I just travel all around the world and find things by intuition.

Likes: Drinking wine. Going to an authentic Japanese bar and having some cocktails.

Dislikes: Someone who writes things in difficult words or talks in a difficult way.

What music do you enjoy listening to? John Dowland, Bach, English traditional folk music and, sometimes, Ozzy Osbourne.

Which authors or books inspire you? *Derek Jarman's Garden*, a book of Andrew Wyeth's paintings, and *RFK Funeral Train* by Paul Fusco.

What are you reading at the moment? I am reading *Fish On* by Ken Kaikou and the Peter Zumthor collection.

ADDRESS BOOK

UK

Baileys
Whitecross Farm
Bridstow
Ross-On-Wye
Herefordshire HR9 6JU
01989 563015
www.baileyshome.com
Our Store – the worn,
weathered and imperfect.

Brook Street Pottery
Hay-On-Wye
Herefordshire HR3 5BQ
01497 821070
info@brookstreetpottery.co.
uk
Studio ceramics and regular
exhibitions.

The Cloth House
47 & 98 Berwick Street
London W1F 8SJ
020 7437 5155
www.clothhouse.com
Ticking, linen and vintage
haberdashery.

Contemporary Ceramics
Centre
63 Great Russell Street
London WC1B 3BF
020 7242 9644
www.cpaceramics.com
Contemporary studio ceramics.

The End
Castle Street
Hay-On-Wye
Herefordshire
07779 788520
Antiques and Hungarian
linen.

Katharine Pole
07747 616692
www.katharinepole.com
French antiques and textiles.

Le Chien et Moi
60 Derby Road
Nottingham NG1 5FD
01159 799199
www.lechienetmoi.com
Homeware.

Material
131 Corve Street
Ludlow
Shropshire SY8 2PG
01584 877952
www.materialmaterial.com
Gallery and bookshop.

Melanie Giles Hairdressing
59 Walcot Street
Bath BA1 5BN
01225 444448
www.melanie-giles.co.uk
Haircuts in an imperfect
setting. Salons in Bath, Frome
and Bradford-On-Avon.

Richards Booth's Bookshop
44 Lion Street
Hay-On-Wye
Herefordshire HR3 5AA
01497 820322
www.boothsbooks.co.uk
Book store, cinema and café.

Robert Young
63 Battersea Bridge Road
London SW11 3AG
020 7228 7847
www.robertyoungantiques.
com
Folk art, furniture and
accessories.

Selvedge
162 Archway Road
London N6 5BB
020 8341 9721
www.selvedge.org
Bi-monthly textiles and crafts
magazine.

Spencer Swaffer Antiques
30 High Street
Arundel
West Sussex BN18 9AB
01903 882132
www.spencerswaffer.co.uk

Summerhill and Bishop
100 Portland Road
London W11 4LQ
020 7229 1337
www.summerhillandbishop.
com
Handcrafted kitchenware.

The Art Shop
8 Cross Street
Abergavenny
Monmouthshire NP7 5EH
01873 852690
www.artshopandgallery.co.uk
Art materials and regular
exhibitions.

Tim Bowen
Ivy House
Ferryside
Carmarthenshire SA17 5SS
01267 267122
www.timbowenantiques.co.uk
Welsh folk art and antiques.

PAINT
Auro Organic Paints
Cheltenham Road
Bisley
Nr Stroud

Gloucestershire GL6 7BX
01452 772020
www.auro.co.uk
Natural emulsions, eggshell
and chalk paints.

Clayworks
Higher Boden Farm
Helston
Cornwall TR12 6EN
01326 341339
www.clay-works.com
Natural pigmented clay
plasters.

Earthborn Paints
Frodsham Business Centre
Bridge Lane
Frodsham
Cheshire WA6 7FZ
01928 734171
www.earthbornpaints.co.uk
Eco-paints.

Little Greene Paint
Company
Wood Street
Manchester M11 2FB
0845 880 5855
www.littlegreene.com

Ty-Mawr Lime
Unit 12 Brecon Business
Park
Brecon
Powys LD3 8BT
01874 611350
www.lime.org.uk
Eco-friendly building materials
and external limewash.

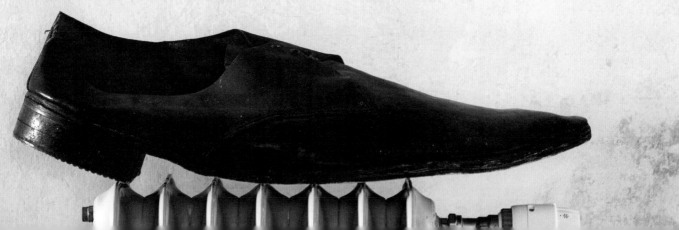

US

The Marston House
Main Street at Middle Street
PO Box 517
Wiscasset
Maine 04578
+1 207 882 6010
www.marstonhouse.com
French antiques and textiles.

ABC Carpet & Home
888 and 881 Broadway
New York, NY 10003
+1 212 473 3000
www.abchome.com
Visit the website for a
retail outlet near you.
*An eclectic collection of
furnishings, linens, rugs,
and other home accessories.*

Altered Antiques
www.altered-antiques.com
*New ways to use old things,
such as furniture crafted from
salvaged wood and metal.*

Anthropologie
www.anthropologie.com
*One-of-a-kind home
accessories, including
decorative hooks, boxes,
cupboard knobs, and racks.*

Historic Houseparts
528–540 South Avenue
Rochester, NY 14620
+1 585 325 2329
www.historichouseparts.com
Salvaged doors, sinks and tiles

John Derian Dry Goods
10 East Second Street
New York, NY 10003
+1 212 677 8408
www.johnderian.com
*Furniture upholstered in
natural linen plus inspiring
antiques, prints and home
accessories*

Olde Good Things
Union Square
5 East 16th Street
New York, NY 10003
+1 212 989 8814
www.ogstore.com
Architectural salvage.

**The Old Fashioned Milk
Paint Company**
436 Main Street
Groton, MA 01450
+1 978 448 6336
www.milkpaint.com
*These paints, made from
natural pigments, replicate the
color and finish of Colonial
and Shaker antiques.*

**Restoration Hardware
935 Broadway**
New York, NY 10010
+1 212 260 9479
www.restorationhardware.com
Visit the website for an
outlet near you.
*Fine hardware, including
lighting, also furniture and
accessories for the home.*

Sylvan Brandt
756 Rothsville Road
Lititz, PA 17543
+1 717 626 4520
www.sylvanbrandt.com
*Reclaimed and weatherboard
flooring, beams, and
architectural antiques.*

PAINT
Earth Pigments
+1 520 682-8928
www.earthpigments.com
*Non-toxic pigments for tinting
lime or clay plaster or concrete*

JAPAN

Ensyu/Buaisou
Ensyu
4-25-8 Daizawa
Setagaya-ku
Tokyo 155–0032
Japan
www.buaisou.com
Accessories.
and
Buaisou
4-25-8 Daizawa
Setagaya-ku
Tokyo 155–0032
Japan
www.buaisou.com
Furniture.

Fog Linen Work
5-35-1 Daita Setagaya
Tokyo 155-0033
www.foglinenwork.com
Household Textiles.

Outbound
2-7-4-101 Kichijoji-Honcho
Musashino
Tokyo 180-0004
Japan
http://outbound.to

Saml.Waltz
http://samlwaltz.com
*Quirky homewares and
exhibitions*
and
Cinq
2f, 2-31-1 Kichijyoji-honcho
Musashino
Tokyo
Japan
http://cinq.tokyo.jp

Starnet
3278-1 Mashiko
Mashiko-cho
Haga-gun
Tochigi 321-4217
Japan
and
Starnet Tokyo
1-3-9 Higashikanda
Chiyoda-ku
Tokyo 101-0031
Japan
http://www.starnet-bkds.com
Destination homeware store.

Zakka
Green Leaves #102
5-42-9 Jingumae
Shibuya-ku
Tokyo 150-0001
Japan
www.2.ttcn.ne.jp/zakka-
tky.com
Stationery and retro goods.

PICTURE CREDITS

All photography by Debi Treloar.

Endpapers The home of Mark & Sally Bailey www.baileyshome.com; **1** Outbound; **2–5** The home of Mark & Sally Bailey www.baileyshome.com; **6** The home of the designer Costanza Algranti in Milan; **7–11** The home of Mark & Sally Bailey www.baileyshome.com; **12** Okura; **13** The home of Mark & Sally Bailey www.baileyshome.com; **14 left** The home of the antique textiles dealer Katharine Pole in London; **14 right** Pip Rau www.piprau.com; **15–16** The home of the antique textiles dealer Katharine Pole in London; **17** The home of Mark & Sally Bailey www.baileyshome.com; **18 above** Pip Rau www.piprau.com; **18 below** The home of the antique textiles dealer Katharine Pole in London; **19** Pip Rau www.piprau.com; **20–21** The home of designer Anna Phillips & Jeff Kightly – owners of knitwear company Hambro & Miller; **22** The home of Mark & Sally Bailey www.baileyshome.com; **23** Ensyu/Buaisou; **24 above** The home of Mark & Sally Bailey www.baileyshome.com; **24 below left** Okura; **24 below right** Fog Linen Work; **25–27** The home of Mark & Sally Bailey www.baileyshome.com; **28 below** Fog Linen Work; **28 above** and **29** The home of Mark & Sally Bailey www.baileyshome.com; **30–31** Noriko Inomoto; **32** The home of Mark & Sally Bailey www.baileyshome.com; **33 above left** and **below left** The home of Mark & Sally Bailey www.baileyshome.com; **33 above centre** and below right Starnet; 33 above right Noriko Inomoto; **33 below centre** Fog Linen Work; **34** Ryuji Mitani; **35** The home of Mark & Sally Bailey www.baileyshome.com; **35** Starnet; **37** The home of Mark & Sally Bailey www.baileyshome.com; **38–45** The home of the antique textiles dealer Katharine Pole in London; **46** Okura; **47–57** The home of Mark & Sally Bailey www.baileyshome.com; **58 above left** Okura; **58 above right** Noriko Inomoto; **58 below** The home of designer Anna Phillips & Jeff Kightly – owners of knitwear company Hambro & Miller; **59** Noriko Inomoto; **60–61** The home of Mark & Sally Bailey www.baileyshome.com; **62–63** The home of designer Anna Phillips & Jeff Kightly – owners of knitwear company Hambro & Miller; **64** Okura; **65 above left**, **above right** and **below left** Ensyu/Buaisou; **65 below right** Pip Rau www.piprau.com; **66 left** Fog Linen Work; **66 right–67** The home of Mark & Sally Bailey www.baileyshome.com; **68** The home of designer Anna Phillips & Jeff Kightly – owners of knitwear company Hambro & Miller; **69 above** and **below right** The home of designer Anna Phillips & Jeff Kightly – owners of knitwear company Hambro & Miller; **69 below left** Ensyu/Buaisou; **70 above** Okura; **70 below** The home of Mark & Sally Bailey www.baileyshome.com; **71 left** Ensyu/Buaisou; **71 right–73** The home of Mark & Sally Bailey www.baileyshome.com; **74–75** Outbound; **76 above left** and below right Outbound; **76 above right** The home of Mark & Sally Bailey www.baileyshome.com; **76 below left** Okura; **77** above left Outbound; **77 above right** The home of the designer Costanza Algranti in Milan; **77 below right** Outbound; **78** Starnet; **79** Outbound; **80–87** The home of the designer Costanza Algranti in Milan; **88** The home of the antique textiles dealer Katharine Pole in London; **89** The home of Mark & Sally Bailey www.baileyshome.com; **90 left** Okura;

90 right Fog Linen Work; **91** Okura; **92 above** Okura; **92 below** Pip Rau www.piprau.com; **93 above left** The home of Mark & Sally Bailey www.baileyshome.com; **93 above right** Okura; **93 below right–94** Fog Linen Work; **95–99** The home of Mark & Sally Bailey www.baileyshome.com; **100 above**, below left and below right The home of Mark & Sally Bailey www.baileyshome.com; **100 below centre** The home of the designer Costanza Algranti in Milan; **101** The home of the antique textiles dealer Katharine Pole in London; **102** Zakka; **103–110** The home of Mark & Sally Bailey www.baileyshome.com; **111** The home of designer Anna Phillips & Jeff Kightly – owners of knitwear company Hambro & Miller; **112–115 above left** The home of Mark & Sally Bailey www.baileyshome.com; **115 above right** The home of designer Anna Phillips & Jeff Kightly – owners of knitwear company Hambro & Miller; **115 below left** Noriko Inomoto; **115 below right–117** The home of Mark & Sally Bailey www.baileyshome.com; **118–125** Pip Rau www.piprau.com; **126** Outbound; **127–128 left** The home of Mark & Sally Bailey www.baileyshome.com; **128 right** Pip Rau www.piprau.com; **129** Ensyu/Buaisou; **130 above left** and **below right** Outbound; **130 above right** The home of Mark & Sally Bailey www.baileyshome.com; **130 below left** Ryuji Mitani; **131 above left** and **below right** Outbound; **131 above right** The home of Mark & Sally Bailey www.baileyshome.com; **132–133** Outbound; **134–135** The home of Mark & Sally Bailey www.baileyshome.com; **136** Masato Hori; **137 above left** The home of Mark & Sally Bailey www.baileyshome.com; **137 above right** Noriko Inomoto; **137 below** Outbound; **138–140** Zakka; **141 above** Wataru Ohashi; **141 below** Zakka; **142** Ensyu/Buaisou; **143** Noriko Inomoto; **144–147 left** The home of Mark & Sally Bailey www.baileyshome.com; **147 right** Noriko Inomoto; **148** Ensyu/Buaisou; **149** The home of Mark & Sally Bailey www.baileyshome.com; **150** Masato Hori; **151** The home of Mark & Sally Bailey www.baileyshome.com; **152** Outbound; **153 above left** Zakka; **153 above right** Ensyu/Buaisou; **153 below left** The home of Mark & Sally Bailey www.baileyshome.com; **153 below right** The home of the designer Costanza Algranti in Milan; **154–163** Ryuji Mitani; **164–165** The home of Mark & Sally Bailey www.baileyshome.com; **166 left** Masato Hori; **166 right** The home of designer Anna Phillips & Jeff Kightly – owners of knitwear company Hambro & Miller; **167** Masato Hori; **168–169** The home of Mark & Sally Bailey www.baileyshome.com; **170 left** Wataru Ohashi; **170–171 above** Pip Rau www.piprau.com; **171 above right** The home of Mark & Sally Bailey www.baileyshome.com; **171 below** The home of the antique textiles dealer Katharine Pole in London; **172–173** The home of Mark & Sally Bailey www.baileyshome.com; **174–176** Masato Hori; **177 above left** The home of designer Anna Phillips & Jeff Kightly – owners of knitwear company Hambro & Miller; **177 above right** Wataru Ohashi; **177 below right** Masato Hori; **178** Masato Hori; **179** Wataru Ohashi; **180–181** The home of Mark & Sally Bailey www.baileyshome.com; **182** Zakka; **183** Okura; **184** The home of Mark & Sally Bailey www.baileyshome.com; **185** Ensyu/Buaisou; **186** Noriko Inomoto; **187 above left** Zakka; **187** above right Fog Linen Work; **187 below** Noriko Inomoto; **188–189** Okura; **190–191** Starnet; **192–201** The weekend home of Shotaro Yoshida and Midori Takahashi in Japan; **202–208** The home of Mark & Sally Bailey www.baileyshome.com.

BUSINESS CREDITS

Key: a = above; b = below;
r = right; l = left; c = centre.

Mark & Sally Bailey
Baileys
Whitecross Farm
Bridstow
Ross-on-Wye
Herefordshire HR9 6JU
www.baileyshome.com
Endpapers, Pages 2–5, 7–11,
13, 17, 22, 24 a, 25–27, 28 a,
29, 32, 33 al, 33 bl , 35, 37,
47–57, 60–61, 66 r, 67, 70 b,
71 r, 72–73, 76 ar, 89, 93 al,
95–99, 100 al,100 ac, 100 ar,
100 bl, 100 br, 103–110,
112–115 al, 115 br, 116–117,
127–128 l, 130 ar, 131 ar,
134–135, 137 al, 144–147
left, 149, 151, 153 bl,
164–165, 168–169, 171 ar,
172–173, 180–181, 184,
202–208.

Costanza Algranti
www.costanzaalgranti.it
Pages 6, 77 ar, 80–87, 100
bc, 153 br.

Ensyu/Buaisou
Ensyu
4-25-8 Daizawa
Setagaya-ku
Tokyo 155–0032
Japan
www.buaisou.com
and
Buaisou
4-25-8 Daizawa
Setagaya-ku
Tokyo 155–0032
Japan
www.buaisou.com
Pages 23, 65 al, 65 al, 65 ar,
65 bl, 69 bl,71 l, 129, 142,
148, 153 ar, 185.

Fog Linen Work
5-35-1 Daita Setagaya
Tokyo 155-0033
T: + 81 3 5481 3728
www.foglinenwork.com
Pages 24 br, 28 b, 33 bc, 66
l, 90 r, 93 br, 94, 187 ar.

Hambro & Miller
www.hambroandmiller.co.uk
Pages 20–21, 58 b, 62–63,
68, 69 a, 69 br, 111, 115 ar,
166 r, 177 al.

Okura
20-11 Satuguku cho
Shibuya-ku
Tokyo 20-11
Japan
www.hrm.co.jp/okura
Pages 12, 24 bl, 46, 58 al,
64, 70 a, 76 bl, 90 l, 91, 92 a,
93 ar, 183, 188–189.

Outbound
2-7-4-101 Kichijoji-Honcho
Musashino
Tokyo
Japan
http://outbound.to
Pages 1, 74–75, 76 al, 76 br,
77 al, 77 br, 79, 126, 130 al,
130 br, 131 ar, 131 br, 132–
133, 137 b, 152.

Persona Studio
2459 Arigasaki Matsumoto
Nagano
Japan
and
10cm
2-4-37 Ote Matsumoto
Nagano
Japan
Pages 34, 130 bl, 154–163.

Katharine Pole
E: info@ katharinepole.com
www.katharinepole.com
Pages 14 l, 15–16, 18 b,
38–45, 88, 101, 171 b.

Noriko Inomoto
Tokyo
Japan
Pages 30–31, 33 ar, 58 ar,
59, 116 bl, 137 ar, 143, 147 r,
186, 187 b.

Pip Rau
E: piprau@mac.com
www.piprau.com
Pages 14 r, 18 a, 19, 65 b, 92
b, 118–125, 128 r, 170, 171 a.

Saml.Waltz
http://samlwaltz.com
and
Cinq
2f, 2-31-1 Kichijyoji-honcho
Musashino
Tokyo
Japan
http://cinq.tokyo.jp
Pages 136, 150, 166 l, 167,
174–176, 177 br, 178.

Starnet
3278-1 Mashiko
Mashiko-cho
Haga-gun
Tochigi 321-4217
Japan
and
Starnet Tokyo
1-3-9 Higashikanda
Chiyoda-ku
Tokyo 101-0031
Japan
http://www.starnet-
bkds.com
Pages 33 ac, 33 br, 36, 78,
190–191.

Tamsier Kuroiso
3–13 Hon-cho
Nasushiobara-shi
Tochigi
325-0056
Japan
Pages 192–201.

Wataru Ohashi
Tokyo
Japan
E: mail@wataruohashi.com
http://wataruohashi.com
Pages 141 a, 170 l, 177 ar,
179.

Zakka
Green Leaves #102
5-42-9 Jingumae
Shibuya-ku
Tokyo 150-0001
Japan
www.2.ttcn.ne.jp/zakka-
tky.com/
Pages 102, 138–140, 141 b,
153 al, 182, 187 al.

ACKNOWLEDGMENTS

This book was a hectic scramble around London, Tokyo, Milan and our home in Herefordshire. We started in Japan with a whirlwind of fourteen locations in six days (and a hurricane in between), staggering under the weight of our bags and photographic equipment. This would have been impossible without the help, generosity and kindness of our friends Yumiko and Wataru. We would also like to thank all the outstanding people who welcomed us with open arms into their Imperfect Homes and looked after us so well.

Massive thanks to everyone at RPS: Cindy, Annabel, Megan, Jess, Leslie and Lauren. Huge thanks to Debi Treloar – simply the best photographer, always so cool and calm. Big thanks to Laura, Kirstin, Cathryn, Donna, Gary, Robyn, Emily and all at Baileys and, last but not least, to the Begwyns and Erwood Film Club.

INDEX

MARK & SALLY BAILEY